Building RESTful Web Services with .NET Core

Developing Distributed Web Services to improve scalability with .NET Core 2.0 and ASP.NET Core 2.0

Gaurav Aroraa
Tadit Dash

BIRMINGHAM - MUMBAI

Building RESTful Web Services with .NET Core

Commissioning Editor: Aaron Lazar
Acquisition Editor: Denim Pinto
Content Development Editor: Anugraha Arunagiri
Technical Editor: Jash Bavishi
Copy Editor: Safis Editing
Project Coordinator: Ulhas Kambali
Proofreader: Safis Editing
Indexer: Mariammal Chettiyar
Graphics: Tania Dutta
Production Coordinator: Shantanu Zagade

First published: May 2018

Production reference: 1290518

Published by Packt Publishing Ltd.
Livery Place
35 Livery Street
Birmingham
B3 2PB, UK.

ISBN 978-1-78829-157-6

www.packtpub.com

To my mother, Late Smt. Santosh, and to the memory of my father, Late Sh. Ramkrishan, for their sacrifices and for exemplifying the power of determination. To my youngest sister Late Baby Kanchan for her love and always being my lucky charm.

– Gaurav Aroraa

To my grandfather late Ganeswar Tripathy, for consistently motivating me.
To my father, Dr. Gobinda Chandra Dash, and mother, Mrs. Sasmita Tripathy, for whatever they have sacrificed in their life to build me.

– Tadit Dash

`mapt.io`

Mapt is an online digital library that gives you full access to over 5,000 books and videos, as well as industry leading tools to help you plan your personal development and advance your career. For more information, please visit our website.

Why subscribe?

- Spend less time learning and more time coding with practical eBooks and Videos from over 4,000 industry professionals

- Improve your learning with Skill Plans built especially for you

- Get a free eBook or video every month

- Mapt is fully searchable

- Copy and paste, print, and bookmark content

PacktPub.com

Did you know that Packt offers eBook versions of every book published, with PDF and ePub files available? You can upgrade to the eBook version at `www.PacktPub.com` and as a print book customer, you are entitled to a discount on the eBook copy. Get in touch with us at `service@packtpub.com` for more details.

At `www.PacktPub.com`, you can also read a collection of free technical articles, sign up for a range of free newsletters, and receive exclusive discounts and offers on Packt books and eBooks.

Contributors

About the authors

Gaurav Aroraa has an M.Phil in computer science. He is a Microsoft MVP, a lifetime member of Computer Society of India (CSI), an advisory member of IndiaMentor, certified as a scrum trainer/coach, XEN for ITIL-F, and APMG for PRINCE-F and PRINCE-P. Gaurav is an open source developer, a contributor to TechNet Wiki, and the founder of Ovatic Systems Private Limited. In 20+ years of his career, he has mentored thousands of students and industry professionals. You can tweet Gaurav on his Twitter handle @g_arora.

To my wife, Shuby Arora, and my angel (daughter), Aarchi Arora, who permitted me to steal time for this book from the time I was supposed to spend with them. Thanks to the entire Packt team, especially Ulhas, Vikas Tiwari, Anugraha Arunagiri, and Jash Bavishi, whose coordination and communication during the period was tremendous, and Denim Pinto, who introduced me for this book.

Tadit Dash is a senior software engineer and a hardcore tech community contributor. Due to his exceptional contribution to the technical community, Microsoft has awarded him with the Microsoft Most Valuable Professional accolade since 2014. CodeProject has awarded him the CodeProject MVP accolade (the first from Odisha). For his constant mentorship, IndiaMentor featured him as a young mentor on their site. He was a featured speaker at DevTechDay Nepal and C# Corner Annual Conference, India. You can follow him on Twitter: @taditdash.

To Utkal Techies Forum members Suvendu Giri, Pravasini Sahoo, Suraj Sahoo, Surya Barik, Abhijit Pattnaik, Sourav Nanda, Jayant Rajwani, Ramesh Barik; my friends Manas Pritam, Deepak Mahapatra; my cousins Lipsa, Aurobin, Titiksha, Juthika, Amrit, Sanvi, Anushka, Swostik; my mentor Gaurav Arora; and the Packt team, Denim Pinto, Vikas Tiwari, Anugraha Arunagiri, and Jash Bavishi.

About the reviewer

Hansamali Gamage is an experienced professional and Microsoft MVP in Visual Studio and Technologies from Sri Lanka. She possesses 5+ years of experience in .NET stack and Azure-related services. She is a frequent speaker at local and global tech events. She is a tech enthusiast and an award-winning writer on the Microsoft Tech Net forum. She works at TIQRI, previously known as Exilesoft, which is technology-focused software engineering company that has offices in Scandinavia, Asia, and Australia.

I would like to thank my loving family for their continuous help and support.

Packt is searching for authors like you

If you're interested in becoming an author for Packt, please visit `authors.packtpub.com` and apply today. We have worked with thousands of developers and tech professionals, just like you, to help them share their insight with the global tech community. You can make a general application, apply for a specific hot topic that we are recruiting an author for, or submit your own idea.

Table of Contents

Preface

This book will take the readers through the design of RESTful web services and leverages the ASP.NET Core Framework to implement these services. Starting from the basics of the philosophy behind REST, the readers will go through the steps of designing and implementing an enterprise-grade RESTful web service. Taking a practical approach, each chapter provides code samples that they can apply to your own circumstances. It brings forth the power of the latest .NET Core release, working with MVC. It then goes beyond the use of the framework to explore approaches to tackle resilience, security, and scalability concerns. The readers will learn techniques to deal with security in Web APIs and discover how to implement unit and integration test strategies. Finally, the book ends by walking you through building a .NET client for your RESTful web service, along with some scaling techniques.

Who this book is for

This book is intended for those who want to learn to build RESTful web services with the latest .NET Core Framework. To make best use of the code samples included in the book, you should have basic knowledge of C# and .NET Core.

What this book covers

Chapter 1, *Getting Started*, will cover the planning phase, explain how to identify a perfect technology stack based on our requirement or problem statements, along with fundamental aspects of RESTful and RESTless services.

Chapter 2, *Build Initial Framework – Layout Foundation of Application*, will get you acquainted with the concepts of various methods, such as GET, POST, PUT, DELETE, and so on.

Chapter 3, *User Registration and Administration*, will get you acquainted with authentication with ASP.NET Core 2.0, Entity Framework Core, Basic Authentication, and OAuth 2.0.

Chapter 4, *Item Catalogue, Cart, and Checkout*, will help you understand the complex components of ASP.NET Core, including .NET Standard 2.0 while building different sections of the e-commerce application.

Chapter 5, *Integrating External Components and Handling*, will help you understand middleware, implementing logging using middleware, authentication, and resource restriction.

Chapter 6, *Testing RESTful Web Services*, will get you acquainted with the test paradigm, testing concepts, stubs and mocking, security testing, and integration testing.

Chapter 7, *Continuous Integration and Continuous Deployment*, will get you acquainted with CI and CD concepts using VSTS and Azure.

Chapter 8, *Securing RESTful Web Services*, will help you understand various security techniques, including basic authentication, XSS attacks, data encryption.

Chapter 9, *Scaling RESTful Services (Performance of Web Services)*, will explain scaling-in, scaling-out, and the various patterns of scaling.

Chapter 10, *Building a Web Client (Consuming Web Services)*, will teach the readers ASP.NET Core and Rest Client with RestSharp.

Chapter 11, *Introduction to Microservices*, gives an overview of microservices by covering ecosystem in microservices with ASP.NET Core.

To get the most out of this book

The reader should have prior knowledge of .NET Core and .NET Standard, along with basic knowledge of C#, RESTful Services, Visual Studio 2017 (as an IDE), Postman, Advanced Rest Client, and Swagger.

To set up the system, readers should have following on their machines:

- Visual Studio 2017 Update 3 or later (for download and installation instructions refer to `https://docs.microsoft.com/en-us/visualstudio/install/install-visual-studio`)
- SQL Server 2008 R2 or later (for download and installation instructions refer to `https://blogs.msdn.microsoft.com/bethmassi/2011/02/18/step-by-step-installing-sql-server-management-studio-2008-express-after-visual-studio-2010/`)

- .NET Core 2.0
  - Download: `https://www.microsoft.com/net/download/windows`
  - Installation instructions: `https://blogs.msdn.microsoft.com/benjaminperkins/2017/09/20/how-to-install-net-core-2-0/`

Download the example code files

You can download the example code files for this book from your account at `www.packtpub.com`. If you purchased this book elsewhere, you can visit `www.packtpub.com/support` and register to have the files emailed directly to you.

You can download the code files by following these steps:

1. Log in or register at `www.packtpub.com`.
2. Select the SUPPORT tab.
3. Click on Code Downloads & Errata.
4. Enter the name of the book in the Search box and follow the onscreen instructions.

Once the file is downloaded, please make sure that you unzip or extract the folder using the latest version of:

- WinRAR/7-Zip for Windows
- Zipeg/iZip/UnRarX for Mac
- 7-Zip/PeaZip for Linux

The code bundle for the book is also hosted on GitHub at `https://github.com/PacktPublishing/Building-RESTful-Web-services-with-DOTNET-Core`. In case there's an update to the code, it will be updated on the existing GitHub repository.

We also have other code bundles from our rich catalog of books and videos available at `https://github.com/PacktPublishing/`. Check them out!

Download the color images

We also provide a PDF file that has color images of the screenshots/diagrams used in this book. You can download it from `https://www.packtpub.com/sites/default/files/downloads/BuildingRESTfulWebServiceswithDOTNETCore_ColorImages.pdf`.

Conventions used

There are a number of text conventions used throughout this book.

`CodeInText`: Indicates code words in text, database table names, folder names, filenames, file extensions, pathnames, dummy URLs, user input, and Twitter handles. Here is an example: "The `Header` must appear as the first child of the envelope, before the body element."

A block of code is set as follows:

```
<?xml version = "1.0"?>
<SOAP-ENV:Envelope
 xmlns:SOAP-ENV = "http://www.w3.org/2001/12/soap-envelope"
 SOAP-ENV:encodingStyle = "http://www.w3.org/2001/12/soap-encoding">
 ...
 SOAP Message information goes here
 ...
</SOAP-ENV:Envelope>
```

When we wish to draw your attention to a particular part of a code block, the relevant lines or items are set in bold:

```
{
  // GET: api/Products
  [HttpGet]
  public IEnumerable<Product> Get()
  {
    return new Product[]
    {
      new Product(1, "Oats", new decimal(3.07)),
      new Product(2, "Toothpaste", new decimal(10.89)),
      new Product(3, "Television", new decimal(500.90))
    };
  }
}
```

Bold: Indicates a new term, an important word, or words that you see onscreen. For example, words in menus or dialog boxes appear in the text like this. Here is an example: "**Simple Object Access Protocol (SOAP)** is an XML-based messaging protocol for exchanging information among computers."

Warnings or important notes appear like this.

 Tips and tricks appear like this.

Get in touch

Feedback from our readers is always welcome.

General feedback: Email feedback@packtpub.com and mention the book title in the subject of your message. If you have questions about any aspect of this book, please email us at questions@packtpub.com.

Errata: Although we have taken every care to ensure the accuracy of our content, mistakes do happen. If you have found a mistake in this book, we would be grateful if you would report this to us. Please visit www.packtpub.com/submit-errata, selecting your book, clicking on the Errata Submission Form link, and entering the details.

Piracy: If you come across any illegal copies of our works in any form on the Internet, we would be grateful if you would provide us with the location address or website name. Please contact us at copyright@packtpub.com with a link to the material.

If you are interested in becoming an author: If there is a topic that you have expertise in and you are interested in either writing or contributing to a book, please visit authors.packtpub.com.

Reviews

Please leave a review. Once you have read and used this book, why not leave a review on the site that you purchased it from? Potential readers can then see and use your unbiased opinion to make purchase decisions, we at Packt can understand what you think about our products, and our authors can see your feedback on their book. Thank you!

For more information about Packt, please visit packtpub.com.

Getting Started

1

Modern web development demands interaction with servers without any hassle. What this means is that with the evolution of different UI and backend frameworks, developers need to find a way of sharing data with any available framework without any dependencies. This means there should be a way of sharing data from the server with clients, irrespective of their language and framework. To bring a uniformity to sharing data, the first thing that comes to mind is `.xml` and `.json`. These formats are supported by every framework.

In this chapter, we will look at an architectural style by which we can get or send data from any program written in any language using any framework. With REST, the architecture we will be discussing, we can bring in methods that can be easily consumed by clients for data operations.

This chapter will cover the following topics:

- RESTful services
- Why should we use RESTful services? The difference between RESTful and RESTless services
- Client-server architecture
- ASP.NET Core and RESTful services

Discussing RESTful services

REST stands for **representational state transfer**. It is an architectural style that defines a set of guidelines for building web services.

What is an architectural style? It's nothing but a concept with predefined principles. We will talk about these principles in a moment. When you follow REST, you are actually implementing the principles that are the building blocks of REST in your application.

However, the implementation of REST will definitely differ from developer to developer. There is no fixed implementation style. Don't get confused with **architectural patterns**, which are not concepts but the actual implementations. MVC is an architectural pattern as it has a fixed structure that defines how the components interact with each other where they can't be differently implemented.

The following is a very simple diagram of a REST-based service:

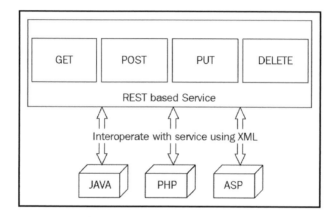

To simplify things, consider the preceding diagram, which shows you a service that has certain methods, such as GET, POST, PUT, and DELETE. That is what this style is all about. When you design your service, which will have all these methods—with the intended operations inside them—we can consider it as a REST-based service, otherwise known as a RESTful service. More importantly, the service can be called from an application built in any platform and language as the service has a standard architecture.

As discussed, a RESTful service is a service that supports REST. Let's talk about the characteristics of REST so that we can understand what is expected from a service that is RESTful.

REST characteristics

The main building blocks of web services are the client and server architectures. The response sent from the server is actually a reply to the client's request. It's like you are asking a question and the server responds if it finds the answer. The response that comes from the server is actually a resource in a certain format or representation. The formats that are usually seen are .json, .xml, .pdf, .doc, and so on.

REST is stateless. **Stateless** means that the state of the system is always different. So, when a request comes to the server, it is served and forgotten. Thus, the next request does not depend on the state of the previous one. Each request is handled by the server independently.

The requests are performed in an HTTP connection. They each take the form of a **uniform resource identifier (URI)**. This identifier helps us to locate the required resource on the web server.

Roy Fielding's PhD dissertation, entitled *Architectural Styles and the Design of Network-Based Software Architectures*, defined REST. The following are some key points extracted from his research:

- Like many distributed architectures, REST imposes layers, statelessness, and caching.
- REST improves efficiency, interoperability, and overall performance.
- REST introduces uniformity by following a set of rules on how to identify and manipulate resources, along with the process to simplify the description about its operations through metadata so that the messages passed will be self-explanatory. We will talk more about this uniformity, which is called the **uniform interface**.
- As REST is an architectural style, a service can be developed using any language or platform as long as it supports HTTP.

 You can read the whole dissertation at `https://www.ics.uci.edu/~fielding/pubs/dissertation/top.htm`.

Resource-oriented architecture

Every resource on the web has been given a unique identifier, otherwise known as a URI. The **uniform resource locator (URL)** is the most common type of URI used on the web today. The URL `https://www.packtpub.com/` identifies and locates the Packt Publishing site.

Let's look at a quick picture of the architecture. In the following diagram, a client is trying to access a resource through an identifier (URL). The resource is present on the server and has a representation that can be returned to the client when requested:

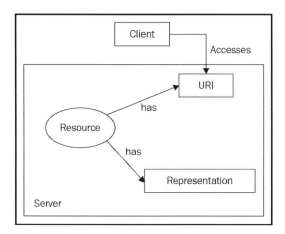

As the name suggests, the URL is something that is tied to only one resource; therefore, if I want to point someone to one resource, I can easily share that identifier in email, chat, and so on.

These identifiers can by easily remembered if they are named with company or resource names. The best example is `www.google.com`, which is very easy to remember as the name Google is present. Therefore, we can spread the resource link by word of mouth and you can enter it into a web browser, such as Chrome or Firefox, within seconds.

You might find hyperlinks on a particular web page that link to another website for another resource. That means that resources are now interconnected because of the hyperlinks.

These interconnected resources form the resource-oriented architecture. Hyperlinks make it easy to navigate from one resource to another by using the target resource URI.

 For example, in HTML, you link to another resource through the anchor element. The following is one anchor element that links to Packt's IoT book catalog page:

```
<a href="https://www.packtpub.com/tech/Internet%20of%20
Things">Packt IoT Books</a>
```

By default, the anchor element is rendered as an underlined text. When you hover over it, you can see the attached URI at the bottom, as shown in the following screenshot:

You can click on the anchor text (**Packt IoT Books**), which then fires a GET request for the target resource URI.

Note that the moment you click the hyperlink, you will land on a web page that is actually a representation of a resource. The most common representation you will encounter is in HTML format. Some other common formats are (X)HTML, JPEG, GIF, WMV, SWF, RSS, ATOM, CSS, JavaScript/JSON, and so on. When a browser receives one of these representations, it tries to parse it and then renders it for viewing, if parsing succeeds.

URI

We have talked a lot about resources. They are actually the pages that we see on a particular website. However, resources in HTTP are not just simple files in the form of HTML web pages. Generally, a resource is defined as any piece of information that can be uniquely identified by a URI, such as `http://packtpub.com/`.

Let's talk about URIs for a moment. A URI consists of a few components: a URI scheme name, such as `http` or `ftp` is the first part, followed by a colon character. After the colon character comes the hierarchical part:

```
<scheme name> : <hierarchical part> [ ? <query> ] [ # <fragment> ]
```

Let's analyze one URI:

```
https://www.flipkart.com/men/tshirts/pr?sid=2oq%2Cs9b%2Cj9y
```

Let's break down the preceding URI:

- The scheme name is `https`.
- The scheme name is followed by the hierarchical part, `//www.flipkart.com/men/tshirts/pr`. The hierarchical part starts with `//`.
- The hierarchical part also contains an optional query, which is `sid=2oq%2Cs9b%2Cj9y`, in this case.

The following is an example of a URI containing the optional fragment part:

```
https://en.wikipedia.org/wiki/Packt#PacktLib
```

REST constraints

REST is defined by six constraints, as shown in the following diagram. One of them is optional:

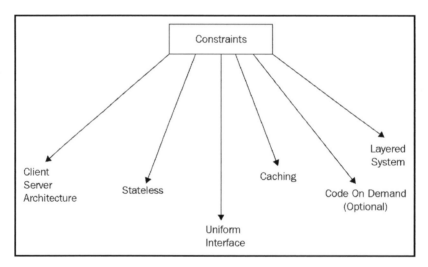

Each of these constraints enforce a design decision for the service that is to be followed. If it is not followed, the service can't be denoted as RESTful. Let's discuss these constraints one by one.

Client-server architecture

The client or the consumer of the service should not worry about how the server processes the data and stores it in the database. Similarly, the server does not need to depend on the client's implementation, especially the UI.

Think of an *internet of things* device or *sensor* that doesn't have much of a UI. However, it interacts with the server to store data using APIs, which are programmed to be fired on specific events. Suppose you are using an IoT device that alerts you when your car runs out of petrol. At the time of a petrol shortage detection by the sensor in the IoT device, it calls the configured API, which then finally sends an alert to the owner.

What that means is that the client and server are not one entity and each can live without the other. They can be designed and evolved independently. Now you might ask, *How can a client work without knowing about the server's architecture, and vice versa?* Well, that is what these constraints are meant for. The service, when interacted with by the clients, provides enough information about its nature: how to consume it, and what operations you can carry out using it.

As we go ahead in this section, you will realize that there is absolutely no relation between the client and the server, and they can be completely decoupled if they adhere to all these constraints perfectly.

Stateless

The term stateless means that the state in which the application remains for a particular time may not persist to the next moment. A RESTful service does not maintain the application's state, and thus it is stateless.

A request in a RESTful service does not depend on a past request. The service treats each request independently. On the other hand, a stateful service needs to record the application's current state when the request is performed so that it can act as required for the next request.

Moreover, because of an absence of these complications, stateless services become very easy to host. As we need not worry about the state of the application, it becomes easy to implement, and maintenance becomes smooth.

Caching

To avoid generating the same data with every request, there is a technique called **caching** that is used to store the data either on the client's or the server's side. This cached data may be used for further reference whenever it is required.

When using caching, it is important that you manage it properly. The reason for this is simple. We are storing data that won't be replaced by fresh data from the server. While this is an advantage that increases the performance of the service, at the same time, if we are not careful as to what to cache and configure during its lifetime, we might end up seeing outdated data. For example, suppose we are showing the live price of gold on our website and we cached this figure. The next time the price changes, it won't be reflected unless we expire the cache that was previously stored.

Let's look at the different kinds of HTTP headers and how to configure caches:

Header	Application
Date	Date and time of the generation of the representation.
Last modified	Date and time when this representation was last modified by the server.
Cache-control	The HTTP 1.1 header used to control caching. We will look at this in more detail after this table.
Expires	This header helps to tag an expiration date and time for this representation.
Age	Denotes the time in seconds since the representation was fetched from the server.

The configuration of the preceding five headers depends upon the nature of the service. Take the example of the service that provides the live price of gold—ideally, it would have the cache age limit as low as possible, or even have caching turned off, because users should see the latest results every time they refer to the site.

However, a site that contains many images would hardly change or update them. In that case, the cache can be configured to store them for a longer duration.

These header values are consulted in accordance with the cache-control header to check whether the cached results are still valid or not.

The following are the most common values for the cache-control header:

Directive	Application
Public	This is the default directive. This allows every component to cache the representation.
Private	Only the client or server can cache the representation. However, intermediary components are restricted.
no-cache/no-store	With this value, we can turn off caching.
max-age	This value is the time in seconds after the date and time is mentioned in the *Date* header, which denotes the validity of the representation.
s-maxage	This does the same as max-age, but only targets intermediary caching.
must-revalidate	This states that the representation must be revalidated if the max-age has passed.
proxy-validate	This does the same as max-revalidate, but only targets intermediary caching.

Code on demand (optional)

As the phrase *code on demand* suggests, the service may try to execute code on the client to extend the functionality. However, this is optional, and not every service does this.

Consider an example of a web application that calls a ticketing service to fetch all the available tickets. The service wants always to show this information in an alert. In order to do this, the service can return a JavaScript code along with the data, which has an alert message with the number of available tickets. Thus, as soon as the client receives the response from the service, an alert is executed and the data is shown.

Uniform interface

When we encounter the word *interface*, the first thing that comes to our mind is decoupling. We create interfaces to have loosely coupled architecture, and the same type of architecture is seen in the case of RESTful.

While implementing REST, we use the same concept to decouple the client from the implementation of the REST service. However, to implement such a decoupling between the client and the service, standards are defined that every RESTful service supports.

Note the word *standard* in the preceding line. We have so many services in the world and, obviously, the consumers outnumber the services. As a result, we have to follow some rules while designing the services because every client should understand the service easily without any hassle.

REST is defined by four interface constraints:

- **Identification of resources**: A URI is used to identify a resource. The resource is a web document.
- **Manipulation of resources through representations**: When a client has a given resource—along with any metadata—they should have enough information to either modify or delete the resource. So, for example, GET means that you want to retrieve data about the URI-identified resource. You can describe an operation with an HTTP method and a URI.
- **Self-descriptive messages**: The messages passed should contain enough information about the data to be understood and processed for further operations. MIME types are used for this purpose.
- **Hypermedia as the engine of the application state (HATEOAS)**: The representation returned from the service should contain all the future actions as links. It is the same as visiting a website in which you find different hyperlinks providing you with the different types of available operations.

HTTP 1.1 provides a set of methods, called verbs. Implementing these verbs in our services would mark them as standardized. The important verbs are as follows:

Method	Operation Performed on Server	Method Type
GET	Read/retrieve a resource.	Safe
PUT	Either insert a new resource or update the resource if it already exists.	Idempotent
POST	Insert a new resource. Can be used to update an existing resource as well.	Nonidempotent
DELETE	Delete a resource .	Idempotent
OPTIONS	Get a list of all the allowed operations for a resource.	Safe
HEAD	Return only the response headers with no response body.	Safe

The preceding table is quite self-explanatory, except the *Method Type* column. Let me clarify this.

A *safe* operation when performed on the service does not have any effect on the original value of the resource. As the GET, OPTIONS, and HEAD verbs only retrieve or read the resource-related stuff and does not update that, they are safe.

An *idempotent (can be repeated)* operation when performed gives the same result no matter how many times we perform it. For example, when you make a DELETE or PUT operation, you are actually operating on a particular resource, and the operation can be repeated with no issues.

 POST versus PUT: This is a very common topic of discussion on the internet, and one that is very easy to understand. Both POST and PUT can be used to insert or update a resource. However, POST is nonidempotent, meaning that it isn't repeatable. The reason is that each time you call using POST, it will create a new resource if you don't provide the exact URI of the resource. The next time you use POST, it will again create a new resource. However, in PUT, it will first validate the existence of the resource. If it exists, it will update it; otherwise, it will create it.

More explanation

Among all the available methods, GET is the most popular one, as it is used to fetch the resource.

The HEAD method will only return the response headers with an empty body. This is mostly only required when we don't need the whole representation of the resource.

The OPTIONS method is used to get a list of the allowed or available operations on the resource.

Consider the following request:

```
OPTIONS http://packtservice.com/Authors/1 HTTP/1.1 HOST: packtservice
```

If the request is authorized and authenticated, it might return something like the following:

```
200 OK Allow: HEAD, GET, PUT
```

The response is actually saying that the service can be called using only all these methods.

Make sure you use the HTTP methods according to their specification. If you design the service to allow GET, but perform a delete operation inside that, then clients will get confused. As they try to GET something, it will actually delete the resource, which is weird.

The following is a request that is made with GET, but it actually deletes the resource inside the server (just imagine):

```
GET http://packtservice.com/DeleteAuthor/1 HTTP/1.1 HOST: packtservice
```

The preceding request might work and delete the resource, but this is not regarded as a RESTful design. The recommended operation would be to use DELETE method to delete a resource like the following:

```
DELETE http://packtservice.com/Authors/1 HTTP/1.1 HOST: packtservice
```

POST versus PUT explained

The use of POST and PUT can be summarized in the following two points:

- PUT is idempotent—it can be repeated, and yields the same result every time. If the resource does not exist, it will create it; otherwise, it will update it.
- POST is nonidempotent—multiple resources will be created if it is called more than once.

The preceding contrast between these verbs is just a general difference. However, there is a very important and significant difference. When using PUT, specifying the complete URI of the resource is necessary. Otherwise, it won't work. For example, the following won't work as it does not specify the exact URI of the author, which can be done by specifying an ID:

```
PUT http://packtservice.com/Authors/
```

To fix this, you can send an ID with this URI using something like the following:

```
PUT http://packtservice.com/Authors/19
created/updated.
```

This means that the author with the ID 19 will be processed, but if that does not exist, it will be created first. Subsequent requests with this URI will be considered as requests to modify the author resource with an ID of 19.

On the other hand, if we do the same with a POST request like the following, it will create a new author resource with the posted data:

```
POST http://packtservice.com/Authors/
```

Interestingly, if you repeat this, you will be responsible for duplicate records with the same data. That is why it is *nonidempotent* in nature.

Note the following request with POST with an ID. Unlike PUT, POST won't consider this for a new resource, if that is does not exist. It will always be treated as an update request:

```
POST http://packtservice.com/Authors/19
updated.
```

The following are the main points to focus on in this section:

- PUT creates or updates one resource, as long as you are calling the same URI
- PUT and POST behave the same, if the resource already exists
- POST, without an ID, will create a resource each time it is fired

Layered system

Most modern applications are designed using multiple layers, and the same is expected from a RESTful service. In a layered system, each layer is restricted to only seeing or knowing the next layer in the hierarchy.

Having a layered architecture helps improve the code's readability, hides complexities, and improves the code's maintainability. Imagine that you have one layer and everything takes place in it, from authentication to database operations. This is absolutely not recommended, as the primary components, such as authentications, business logic, and database operations, are not separated out.

Thus, this constraint is expected from a RESTful service, and no client can actually say that it is connected to the final layer.

Advantages and disadvantages of RESTful services

The following are some advantages and disadvantages of RESTful services:

Advantages

The advantages of using RESTful services are as follows:

- No dependency on a platform or any programming language
- Standardized methods through HTTP

- It doesn't store the state of the clients on the server
- Supports caching
- Accessible to any type of client, such as mobile, web, or desktop

Disadvantages

While there are advantages, there must be some cons. Let's look at some disadvantages of RESTful services:

- If the standards are not followed correctly, they are difficult for clients to understand
- Documentation becomes problematic as no such metadata is provided
- Security is a concern, if no such process is followed to restrict the access of resources

ASP.NET Core and RESTful services

.NET Core is defined as a cross-platform, open-source, cloud-ready, and modular .NET platform for creating modern web apps, microservices, libraries, and console applications that run everywhere (Windows, Linux, and macOS).

ASP.NET Core is a free and open-source web framework, and the next generation of ASP.NET. It is a modular framework consisting of small packages of framework components that run on both the full .NET Framework, Windows, and the cross-platform .NET Core.

The framework is a complete rewrite from the ground up. It unites the previously separate ASP.NET MVC and ASP.NET Web API into a single programming model.

ASP.NET Web API has been built to map the web/HTTP programming model to the .NET Framework programming model. It uses familiar constructs, such as Controller, Action, Filter, and so on, which are used in ASP.NET MVC.

ASP.NET Web API is designed on top of the ASP.NET MVC runtime, along with some components that simplify HTTP programming. We can leverage Web API technology to perform actions on the server with .NET Framework; however, to be RESTful, we should adhere to the standards that we discussed earlier in this chapter. Fortunately, Web API automatically manages all the low-level transport details of HTTP while maintaining all the required constraints.

Because of the uniformity that Web API provides, enforcing the RESTful principles, clients such as mobiles, web applications, the cloud, and so on can easily access it without any problem:

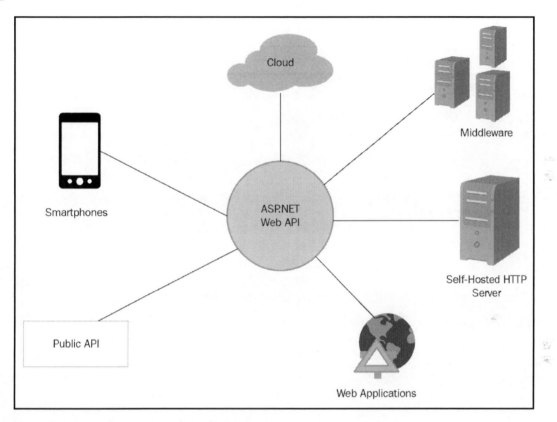

Prior to ASP.NET Core, MVC and Web API were different as they inherited `Controller` and `ApiController` classes respectively. On the other hand, in ASP.NET Core, they follow the same structure.

The following is the Solution Explorer view of both MVC and Web API. You can see that they have a similar structure:

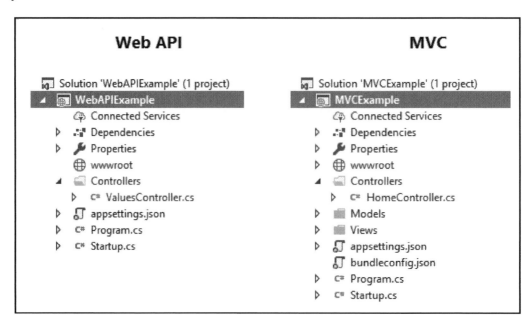

The following is a controller that was automatically created when I clicked on **File | New | Project | ASP.NET Core Web Application | Web API**. You can see the base class of the controller is `Controller` instead of `ApiController`:

```
namespace WebAPIExample.Controllers
{
  [Route("api/[controller]")]
  public class ValuesController : Controller
  {
    // GET api/values
    [HttpGet]
    public IEnumerable<string> Get()
    {
      return new string[] { "value1", "value2" };
    }
    // GET api/values/5
    [HttpGet("{id}")]
    public string Get(int id)
    {
      return "value";
    }
    // POST api/values
```

```
    [HttpPost]
    public void Post([FromBody]string value)
    { }
    // PUT api/values/5
    [HttpPut("{id}")]
    public void Put(int id, [FromBody]string value)
    { }
    // DELETE api/values/5
    [HttpDelete("{id}")]
    public void Delete(int id)
    {  }
  }
}
```

Don't worry about codes now; we will discuss everything later in this book.

Summary

REST defines how to use the uniform interface through additional constraints, how to identify resources, how to manipulate resources through representations, and how to include metadata that makes messages self-describing.

The web is built on HTTP's uniform interface, and the focus is on interacting with resources and their representations. REST isn't tied to any specific platform or technology; the web is the only major platform that fully embodies REST. The basic style of the architecture of RESTful web services is client–server.

Here, the client requests a resource and the server processes and responds to the requested resource. The response of the server is user-based and platform-independent. The separation of concerns is the principle behind the client–server constraints. Because in client–server architecture, the storage and user interfaces are roles taken by the server and client respectively, it has improved portability of the user interface across multiple platforms.

We should document every resource and URI for client developers. We can use any format for structuring our document, but it should contain enough information about resources, URIs, available methods, and any other information required for accessing the service.

Swagger is a tool that can be used for documentation purposes, and provides all the information regarding the API endpoints on one screen, where you can visualize the API and test it by sending parameters as well. Developers can use another tool called *Postman* for testing out APIs. Both of these tools will be explained with examples in the upcoming chapters of this book.

ASP.NET Web API is a development environment constructed to develop RESTful web services that allow applications to send and receive HTTP requests (*web requests*) easily and perform operations based on the types of requests that are made to it (such as providing information about a user when given their ID, and so on).

Web API design in ASP.NET Core has been simplified following the same programming model as MVC.

In the next chapter, we will start coding by setting up the environment and look into the various fundamentals of the HTTP verbs in Web API.

Building the Initial Framework – Laying the Foundation of the Application

2

In the last chapter, we talked about REST, its characteristics, and how it is implemented in ASP.NET Core. We will go ahead with that knowledge and set up the environment to develop an application in this chapter.

We will start building the basic framework of the app. We will understand each and every HTTP verb, how they work, and their implementation paradigms in ASP.NET Core Web API. Before all that, we will have a quick look at SOAP and how it is different from REST.

While we walk though the verbs, we will explore a very easy-to-use tool to analyze the HTTP requests and responses.

We will cover the following topics:

- All about web services (REST and SOAP)
- Running the development server
- REST verbs and status codes
- Implementation of verbs in ASP.NET Core Web API
- Examples using Postman
- SOAP versus REST
- Single-page application model with REST API
- Service-oriented architecture (SOA) overview with REST

SOAP

Simple Object Access Protocol (SOAP) is an XML-based messaging protocol for exchanging information among computers. SOAP relies on application layer protocols, most often **Hypertext Transfer Protocol (HTTP)** or **Simple Mail Transfer Protocol (SMTP)**, for message negotiation and transmission. As we are talking about HTTP, which is installed and runs on every operating system, web services implementing SOAP can be called from any platform using any language.

SOAP structure

We already know that a SOAP message is an XML document, but let's have a better look by way of a diagram:

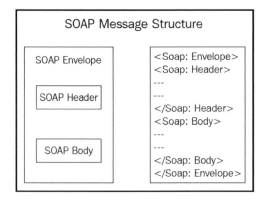

The following is a description of the components from the preceding diagram:

- **Envelope**: Mandatory element of SOAP message structure. Defines the start and the end of the message.
- **Header**: Optional element of the SOAP message. It contains information regarding the SOAP message that can be used to process the data.
- **Body**: This is the main part, which contains the actual message in XML structure. Obviously, it is a mandatory element.
- **Fault**: If any errors occur while processing the SOAP message, an optional Fault element can be used to provide information about them.

You must be thinking who exactly told us to follow this type of structure. Well, there is an organization named W3 that proposes standards for particular technologies. They have done the same for the SOAP structure.

You can easily find details about the SOAP envelope at http://www.w3.org/2001/12/soap-envelope. Likewise, you can see details about SOAP encoding and data types at http://www.w3.org/2001/12/soap-encoding.

 Whatever we discuss about the structure of the SOAP message is defined by the W3 organization. However, this organization constantly investigates ways to optimize structures and bring in more robust specifications from time to time. So, we have to update with the latest specifications provided by them and implement them accordingly.

The following block depicts the general structure of a SOAP message:

```
<?xml version = "1.0"?>
<SOAP-ENV:Envelope xmlns:SOAP-ENV =
"http://www.w3.org/2001/12/soap-envelope"
 SOAP-ENV:encodingStyle = "http://www.w3.org/2001/12/soap-encoding">
  <SOAP-ENV:Header>
    ...
    ...
  </SOAP-ENV:Header>
  <SOAP-ENV:Body>
    ...
    ...
    <SOAP-ENV:Fault>
      ...
      ...
    </SOAP-ENV:Fault>
    ...
  </SOAP-ENV:Body>
</SOAP_ENV:Envelope>
```

The receiver is notified about the whole SOAP message with the indication of an envelope. What this means is, if the message received by the client has an envelope inside it, then the message is completely received and the client can parse and use it for further processing. Thus, the SOAP envelope plays the role of packaging the whole message.

Important points about SOAP

The following are some important points about SOAP:

- Envelope in every SOAP message has the root position and that is mandatory for all SOAP messages.
- Exactly one body element should be present inside one SOAP envelope.

- The `Header` element is an optional element. However, if that is present, then there should be only one `Header` element.
- The `Header` must appear as the first child of the envelope, before the body element.
- The `ENV` namespace prefix and the `Envelope` element are used in order to build one SOAP envelope. (Refer to the following example.)
- The `encodingStyle` attribute defines the data types used in the document. This gives a generalization of the data types that appear in the message. If this attribute appears on any SOAP element, it will apply the encoding rules to the element's contents and all child elements.

The following is an example of a v1.2-compliant SOAP message:

```
<?xml version = "1.0"?>
<SOAP-ENV:Envelope
 xmlns:SOAP-ENV = "http://www.w3.org/2001/12/soap-envelope"
 SOAP-ENV:encodingStyle = "http://www.w3.org/2001/12/soap-encoding">
 ...
 SOAP Message information goes here
 ...
</SOAP-ENV:Envelope>
```

SOAP with HTTP POST

The `Authors` mentioned in the HTTP header is actually the URL of the controller or program to be invoked that have a `POST` action method inside it. Everything is hosted at www.packtpub.com.

```
POST /Authors HTTP/1.1
Host: www.packtpub.com
Content-Type: application/soap; charset="utf-8"
Content-Length: nnnn

<?xml version = "1.0"?>
<SOAP-ENV:Envelope
xmlns:SOAP-ENV = "http://www.w3.org/2001/12/soap-envelope"
SOAP-ENV:encodingStyle = " http://www.w3.org/2001/12/soap-encoding">
 ...
  Message information goes here
 ...
</SOAP-ENV:Envelope>
```

REST

REST is an architectural style for providing standards between computer systems on the web, so that systems can communicate with each other easily. Services compliant to the REST style are often called RESTful services.

Let's talk about a few important constraints of a web service when it is tagged as RESTful.

Server and client are independent

With REST, there is no restriction or dependency between server and client. Both can be independent of each other. It's just the URL by which the client understands the service. The code for a web service on a server can be modified without caring about the clients that are associated with it and vice versa.

This kind of separation helps the client/server architecture to breathe freely without any hurdles. Therefore, designing the application and separating its core business logic becomes easy. What I mean by that is simple. Designing the app can be done using client-side technologies and the RESTful web service is invoked wherever there is a necessity for business-related operations in a database.

However, keeping both server and client modular and separate depends on one condition and that is the format of the messages they send and receive. Both of them should be aware of the message format to send and receive.

As the user interface is separated from the business-and data-storage-related operations, flexibility and scalability can be improved by simplifying the server components. Moreover, the separation allows each component to evolve independently.

REST endpoints are exposed by certain URLs. Different clients can connect using the URL, then perform the action intended and get the response back.

In this book, we will build a small e-commerce web service with minimal operations, where a user can use a cart and make orders. These operations will be exposed using endpoints. As we discussed, endpoints can be easily consumed from different types of clients including mobile apps, web apps, server-side code, and so on.

Statelessness

The concept is very easy to understand. In a server/client architecture, the server needs to know which client is requesting data from it and, accordingly, it decides what to send and what not to send.

However, REST systems are stateless. That means the server does not need to know anything about the client's state and vice versa. That would eventually remove the overhead on the server to identify the client each time a request comes in.

But now the question is, how do the client and server interact? The answer is through appropriate messages. Suppose a user wants to see one order detail. It would simply ask the server by sending the ID of the order and the server would return the order details in either `.json` or `.xml` format, which can be easily parsed by the client. Every message has the required information for how to deal with that.

These constraints (along with a few other constraints such as *caching, layered system, uniform interface,* and *code on demand*) when implemented on a web service help RESTful applications achieve reliability, optimized performance, and scalability. The reason being that components can be managed independently, updated flawlessly, and reused without affecting the system as a whole.

Let's look at exactly how communication takes place between the server and client in the next section.

Setting up the environment

Before we explore the communication mechanism, let's first set up the development environment. We will use Visual Studio 2017 for our examples.

Open Visual Studio and undertake our favorite step, **File | New | Project**, which opens up a dialog window with available templates, as shown in the following screenshot:

Select **ASP.NET Core Web Application** as shown in the preceding screenshot. Don't forget to select **.NET Core** in the left-hand side panel. Everything looks cool now.

Let's click **OK** and then we will land on another dialog where we can select more templates related to our web app. Obviously, we will click on **Web API** and then click **OK**.

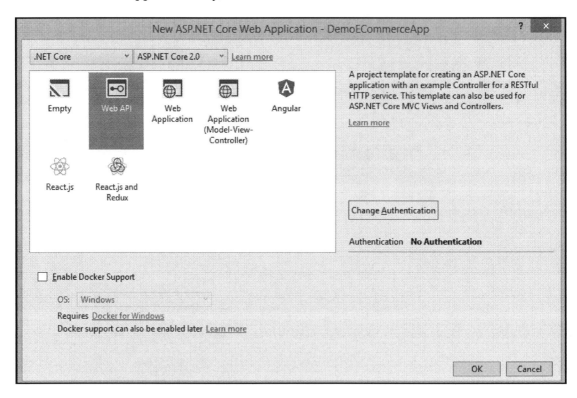

The project is created. Beautifully, it has crafted all the necessary components and created an example controller for us named `ValuesController` as shown in the following screenshot:

Now, here is one interesting fact. Notice that the `ValuesController` class inherits the `Controller` base class. If you were familiar with Web API in ASP.NET before Core, you might know that the base class was `ApiController` instead. The reason behind this change is to have a uniformity between API and MVC structures. `Controller` was the base class in ASP.NET MVC. Now in ASP.NET Core, both MVC and Web API templates inherit the same base class. With ASP.NET Core, MVC and Web API are merged into one programming model.

Running the application

To make sure everything is working fine, let's run the application.

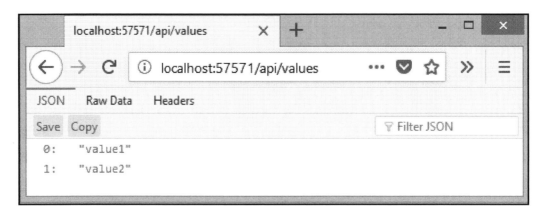

Let's discuss what has just happened in the following sections.

What's cooking here?

Notice the URL, `localhost:57571/api/values`, which sends the request to `ValuesController` because the route defined over the controller is `[Route("api/[controller]")]`. By convention, the controller name is always appended with the text **Controller**. Thus `api/values` hits `ValuesController`.

Now the question is, how it returns `value1` and `value2`. That is because we directly accessed the URL through the browser, which ultimately sent a `GET` request to the controller. As the controller already has a `Get` method, it got executed. The `Get` method is as follows:

```
// GET api/values
[HttpGet]
public IEnumerable<string> Get()
{
   return new string[] { "value1", "value2" };
}
```

This method returns an array of strings, which is printed in the browser. For understanding, the URL format is already there above the method (`api/values`).

Interesting facts

Let's experiment with a few things now. You will get a very good insight into what happens behind the scenes:

1. Add another method, `Get12()`, to the controller and remove the `[HttpGet]` method:

```
public IEnumerable<string> Get12()
{
  return new string[] { "value1", "value2", "value3" };
}
// GET api/values
//[HttpGet] - Remove this attribute
public IEnumerable<string> Get()
{
  return new string[] { "value1", "value2" };
}
```

What do you think the output would be? It's interesting. Here is the output:

That means it found two GET methods and it was not able to decide which one to execute. Note that neither of them is decorated by an attribute, such as `[HttpGet]`.

2. Now let's plan to bring back the attribute and test what happens. However, we will decorate the new `Get12` method and leave the old `Get` method intact with the attribute commented. So, the code would be:

```
[HttpGet]
public IEnumerable<string> Get12()
{
  return new string[] { "value1", "value2", "value3" };
}
```

```
// GET api/values
//[HttpGet]
public IEnumerable<string> Get()
{
   return new string[] { "value1", "value2" };
}
```

Let's have a quick look at what we did to the output:

Clear enough! The Get12 method was executed and the reason for this was that we explicitly told it that it was the Get method by way of the [HttpGet] attribute.

3. More fun can be experienced by adding an attribute to both of the methods:

```
[HttpGet]
public IEnumerable<string> Get12()
{
   return new string[] { "value1", "value2", "value3" };
}
// GET api/values
[HttpGet]
public IEnumerable<string> Get()
{
   return new string[] { "value1", "value2" };
}
```

Can you guess the output? Yes, it is the same as we saw when we had both methods without the attribute **AmbiguousActionException** as shown in the following screenshot:

4. Finally, let's have another method named `HelloWorld()` with the attribute along with the existing ones. Let's remove the attributes from the other ones:

```
[HttpGet]
public string HelloWorld()
{
   return "Hello World";
}
public IEnumerable<string> Get12()
{
   return new string[] { "value1", "value2", "value3" };
}
// GET api/values
public IEnumerable<string> Get()
{
   return new string[] { "value1", "value2" };
}
```

Perfect! Let's see the output. It's **Hello World** in the browser:

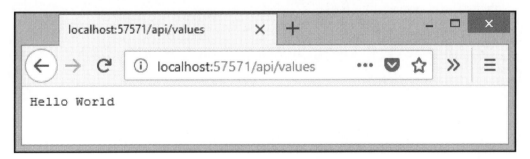

Conclusions

The following conclusions can be made from the preceding observation. Note that we are talking about GET requests with the URL api/values, which means we are talking about all nonparameterized action methods in the controller. While reading the following points, ignore methods with parameters or other attributes:

- When we access a particular Web API controller without any parameters (for example, api/values), action methods with the [HttpGet] attribute are searched first from the controller.
- If an attribute is not mentioned in nonparameterized methods, then the .NET Core runtime will get confused when selecting one action method for the request.
- There is no restriction on the naming convention of the action method. As long as it is the only method with no [HttpGet] attribute or the only method with an [HttpGet] attribute, it would be perfectly executed when GET request comes to the API.

Request and response

Now that we have had a quick look at the demo ValuesController, let's examine exactly how the client sends the request and how it receives the response.

A REST request generally consists of the following:

- **HTTP verb:** This denotes what kind of operation the requests want to perform on the server.
- **Header:** This element of the REST request allows the client to pass more information about the request.
- **URL:** The actual path to the resource that the REST request wants to operate on.
- **Body:** The body can contain extra data related to a resource to identify or update it. This is optional though.

HTTP verbs

The following are basic HTTP verbs used while requesting a REST system for resource interaction:

- **GET:** Used to retrieve a specific resource by its identity or a collection of resources
- **POST:** Used to create/insert a new resource
- **PUT:** Used to update a specific resource by its identity
- **DELETE:** Used to remove a specific resource by its identity

Let's try to explore the request/response mechanism in REST for these verbs one by one. We will try to design an e-commerce application with basic operations. In the first phase, we will work on products, which is the core of these types of apps.

Postman

To test the API, we can use a very easy-to-use tool named *Postman*. It can be downloaded from: `https://www.getpostman.com/`. Please download and open it. We will see how to send requests through Postman and analyze responses we get from Web API in the next section.

GET

I will add another controller called `ProductsController`. For now, let's have a simple action method, `GET`, which will return some products. The products are hard-coded in the action method for now. The method will look like the following:

```
using Microsoft.AspNetCore.Mvc;
using System.Collections.Generic;
namespace DemoECommerceApp.Controllers
{
  [Produces("application/json")]
  [Route("api/[Controller]")]
  public class ProductsController : Controller
  {
    // GET: api/Products
    [HttpGet]
    public IEnumerable<Product> Get()
    {
      return new Product[]
      {
```

```
            new Product(1,  "Oats", new decimal(3.07)),
            new Product(2,  "Toothpaste", new decimal(10.89)),
            new Product(3,  "Television", new decimal(500.90))
        };
      }
    }
  }
```

The `[Route]` attribute is provided with a well-defined template of `"api/[Controller]"`. Here, the controller name is `ProductsController`. When we request using the URL `api/Products`, the framework will search for a controller with that route defined on it. The `[Controller]` placeholder is a special naming convention that will be replaced with the text (name of controller) `Products` at runtime. However, you can directly write the fully qualified template with the controller name, such as `[Route (api/Products)]`.

So, this GET method will return us three products with their details. The `Product` class can be designed, like the following, with a constructor to build *Product* objects:

```
public class Product
{
  public Product(int id, string name, decimal price)
  {
    Id = id;
    Name = name;
    Price = price;
  }
  public int Id { get; set; }
  public string Name { get; set; }
  public decimal Price { get; set; }
}
```

We are done. Let's do a GET request through *Postman* to analyze the request and response mechanism in REST. For a GET request, it's simple. Just open Postman. Then follow the steps mentioned in the following screenshot:

Executing GET request in Postman

In **Step-1**, just paste the URL, which is http://localhost:57571/api/products for our example. Everything else is already set for a GET request. You can see the request type to the left of the URL box, which is GET. That means the current request will be a GET request. Hit the **Send** button as shown in **Step-2**.

The response is a list of products shown inside the section at the bottom. It's in .json format. Please refer to the following screenshot, which displays the response of the GET request:

Now that you have had a pleasant look at how GET works, let's analyze what happens behind the scenes. The client, which is *Postman* here, sends an HTTP request and gets a response in return. While sending requests it also specifies the Request Headers, and the server, in return, sends the Response Headers.

HTTP Headers enable the client and server to both send and receive additional information with the request and response respectively. This decides the exact behavior of the HTTP transaction. You can refer to the following resources to learn more about the headers. We will have a quick look at the headers in the next section:

- https://www.w3.org/Protocols/rfc2616/rfc2616-sec14.html
- https://developer.mozilla.org/en-US/docs/Web/HTTP/Headers

In Postman, you can click on **Code,** as shown in the following screenshot:

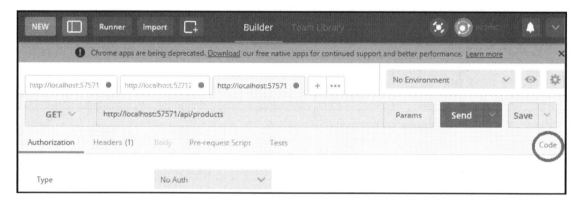

Clicking on this link will open one modal that will show you the HTTP Request Headers sent to the server to serve the request. Check out the following screenshot of the modal, which clearly mentions the Request Type as GET, Host as the URL of the API, and then other headers such as Cache-Control and Postman-Token:

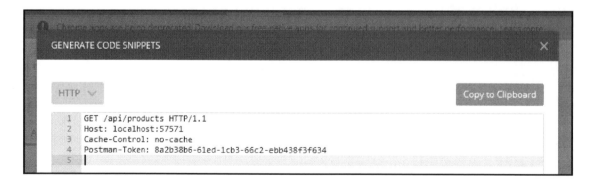

Want to know what the *jQuery* code snippet looks like for this GET call? It's super-easy with Postman. Click on **Code** on the main screen, then from the drop-down menu containing languages, select **jQuery**. (See the following screenshot.) Moreover, you can get code in different languages by selecting from the drop-down list. Happy copying!

GENERATE CODE SNIPPETS

```
JavaScript Jquery AJAX                                    Copy to Clipboard

 1 ▾ var settings = {
 2      "async": true,
 3      "crossDomain": true,
 4      "url": "http://localhost:57571/api/products/",
 5      "method": "GET",
 6 ▾    "headers": {
 7        "cache-control": "no-cache",
 8        "postman-token": "bcf0f3d4-7ed7-012f-06fc-5b373ddb299e"
 9      }
10    }
11
12 ▾ $.ajax(settings).done(function (response) {
13      console.log(response);
14    });
```

Response Header is clearly shown on the main page, as shown in the following screenshot. Notice that there is a **Status** code mentioned, which is **200 OK** in this case. So, what does this code signify?

Let's talk about it in the next section.

Postman Response Headers

Status codes

When a server returns responses, it includes status codes. These status codes inform the client how the request performed on the server. As a developer, you do not need to know every status code (there are many of them), but you should know the most common ones and how they are used:

Status Code	Explanation
200 OK	Standard response for successful HTTP requests.
201 CREATED	Standard response for an HTTP request when an item is successfully created.
204 NO CONTENT	Standard response for successful HTTP requests, if nothing is returned in the response body.
400 BAD REQUEST	Request cannot be processed because of bad request syntax, excessive size, or another client error.
403 FORBIDDEN	Client does not have permission to access the requested resource.
404 NOT FOUND	Resource could not be found at this time. It might have been deleted, or does not exist yet.

500 INTERNAL SERVER ERROR	This response comes whenever there is a failure or exception happens while processing the server side codes.

Some status codes are (by default) expected from the server for the following HTTP verbs:

- GET: Returns **200 OK**
- POST: Returns **201 CREATED**
- PUT: Returns **200 OK**
- DELETE: Returns **204 NO CONTENT** if the operation failed

We already saw how API returned **200 OK** for the GET request. As we move forward with other verbs, we will explore the responses returned with the codes mentioned previously.

ASP.NET Core HTTP attributes

According to the *Internet Engineering Task Force (IETF) RFC-7231* document (`https://tools.ietf.org/html/rfc7231`), ASP.NET Core has implemented seven HTTP attributes out of the eight HTTP verbs listed. The only exclusion in the framework, from the list of verbs, is the HTTP TRACE verb.

Following is the complete list of HTTP verb attributes that are provided in ASP.NET Core:

- HttpGetAttribute
- HttpPostAttribute
- HttpPutAttribute
- HttpDeleteAttribute
- HttpHeadAttribute
- HttpPatchAttribute
- HttpOptionsAttribute

As the verb name is attached with the attribute, it is very obvious that they will be used for their respective verbs. These attributes help the framework to understand what action method is associated with what verb. With that in mind, it can decide which one to execute when a request comes for the controller.

Another important attribute for routing is also provided by the framework, named `RouteAttribute`.

There are a few more attributes used for the parameters of action methods to help recognize parameters passed to the API action from different places of the request such as URL, Body, and so on. Following are some attributes present in the framework for the action parameters:

- `FromServicesAttribute`
- `FromRouteAttribute`
- `FromQueryAttribute`
- `FromBodyAttribute`
- `FromFormAttribute`

POST

POST is used to create a resource. In our case, we will try to create a product using a POST request to the server. Before doing that, we will make a few changes to our project. You can find all related code on GitHub (`https://github.com/PacktPublishing/Building-RESTful-Web-services-with-DOTNET-Core`), so don't worry at all!

Why wait then? Let's write the Post method as follows:

```
// POST: api/Products
[HttpPost]
public async Task<IActionResult> Post([FromBody]Product product)
  => (await _productService.CreateProductAsync(product))
    ? (IActionResult)Created($"api/products/{product.Id}", product) // HTTP
201
    : StatusCode(500); // HTTP 500
```

The action method calls `CreateProductAsync` of the related service and checks if the operation was successful. If successful, it sends back `201`, else `500`. Note that to send back the correct status code, we are leveraging the `IActionResult`. This interface has a large set of subclasses that are accessible via the `Controller` class. Since we inherit from the `Controller` base class, we can easily use methods such as `StatusCode` to return our intended status according to the operation we performed on the resource.

In the previous section, we mentioned that on `POST` success, we should get **201 CREATED** and on failure, it should send a generalized **500 Internal Server Error** response. That is what the code does.

There is another interesting thing, that is: `Created($"api/products/{product.Id}"`, `product)`. This is a method inside the `Controller` class which assigns the URL to the location and 201 to the status code of the response. Don't believe me!? Okay, let me prove it by way of *Postman*, right away.

Have a look at the following screenshot taken from the *Postman* request screen:

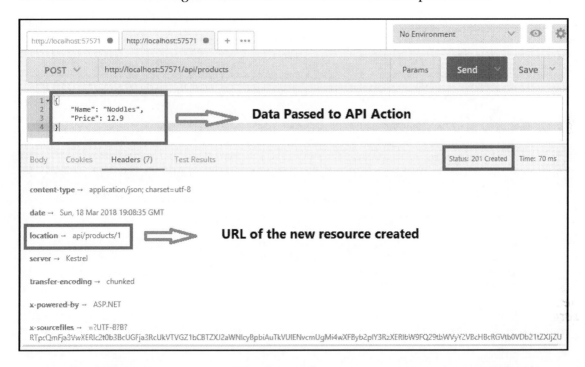

Notice that we passed the data for a product as JSON and after creating the product, the API returned us the status code as **201 Created** and the URL of the new product created, which is **api/products/1**. What that means is that when you run this URL as a GET request, you will receive the newly created product details. Simple, isn't it?

As you can see, the datatype of the passed product details is JSON, but the question is, who told the server that it is in that format? Well, that's the request header `content-type` set with value `application/json`. You can see that in the last screenshot. A default encoding of `charset=utf-8` is appended by *Postman*.

However, interestingly, how come *Postman* knew that we wanted the datatype content to be JSON? It can't set it automatically. I told it to do that.

The option to set any type of request header is just below the URL textbox. Refer to the following screenshot, which shows that I have set the `content-type` header:

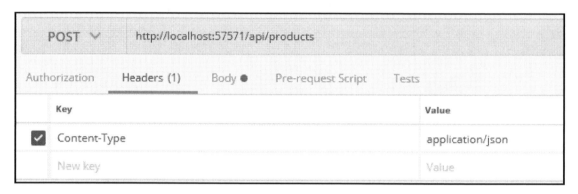

For the previously mentioned GET request, which returns the product details by ID, we can design the action method as follows:

```
// GET: api/Products/1
[HttpGet("{id}")]
public Task<Product> Get(int id)
    => _productService.GetOrderAsync(id);
```

Here, we are providing a template argument of `"{id}"` to [HttpGet]. This will make sure that one HTTP Get route such as `api/orders/1` is available—where the ID is a variable passed to the GET request.

> We have a service called `ProductService` which is implementing the interface `IProductService` and through the constructor of the controller, the service (dependency) is injected, which is called *dependency injection*. With .NET Core, it's very easy to handle dependencies with the built-in *inversion of control container*. If you are not getting what I am talking about, then I would highly recommend going through my other book on this topic, *Dependency Injection in .NET Core* (`https://www.packtpub.com/application-development/dependency-injection-net-core-20`).

PUT

The HTTP PUT verb is idempotent. This means that the first HTTP PUT request with a certain payload will impact the server and the resource. It will update the resource specified by ID. However, subsequent HTTP PUT requests with the same payload would result in the same response as the first one.

Consider the following example where we will update one product:

```
// PUT: api/Products/1
[HttpPut("{id}")]
public async Task<IActionResult> Put(int id, [FromBody]Product product)
   => (await _productService.UpdateProductAsync(id, product))
     ? Ok()
     : StatusCode(500);
```

The [HttpPut] attribute is supplied with a template of {id} similar to what we had in [HttpGet]. In the case of PUT, it would get the ID from the URL and the Product object from the body of the request, which is specified by the [FromBody] attribute as we did in the case of POST in the previous section.

When the ID and the product object is tied with the arguments, the method body starts execution, which in turn calls the service method UpdateProductAsync with the same parameters. That method would return a Boolean based on whether the update was successful. If everything was successful, we would return **200 OK** by calling the OK() method, otherwise a **500 Internal Server Error** would be given if an error occurred.

Let me show you the screenshot from Postman:

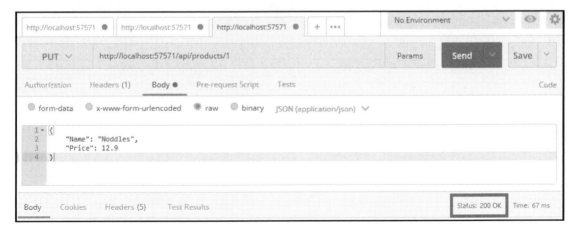

Another status code, **301 Moved Permanently**, can be returned if the PUT request comes with an ID that has expired, meaning the product passed in the request body is not associated with the ID. To identify this condition, we need to add business logic accordingly, and if we can verify whether the ID is related to the product or not. If not, we can simply return **301 Moved Permanently** with the new URL where the product actually exists currently.

DELETE

Ideally, a DELETE request should delete the resource. Once the operation is successful, we can send a **200 OK** status code by calling the OK() method.

Refer to the following code block:

```
// DELETE: api/Products/1
[HttpDelete("{id}")]
public async Task<IActionResult> Delete(int id)
   => (await _productService.DeleteOrderAsync(id))
     ? (IActionResult)Ok()
     : NoContent();
```

Notice the DeleteOrderAsync method, which is provided with the ID of the product to delete. Now, you can return a Boolean from that method, which will indicate whether the operation was successful or not. If you don't find any product for that ID, simply return false. Then, we will decide what to return to the client accordingly.

If you return false, NoContent() can be used to return status code *204*. If the resource is already deleted and the client is requesting the same, then the server will return a status code **204 No Content**. That means the server is not able to find the requested resource as it does not exist anymore.

Have a look at the Postman screenshot. See the **Status** code is **200 OK** for a successful delete:

SOAP versus REST

Following are some key differences between SOAP and REST:

SOAP	REST
It is an XML-based message protocol.	It is an architectural style.
WSDL is used for communication between client and server.	XML or JSON is used to send and receive data between client and server.
Services are invoked by calling the RPC method.	Services expose endpoints via URLs.
Response is easily readable by a human.	Response is readable in the form of plain XML or JSON.
Data transfer occurs over HTTP. It leverages protocols such as SMTP, FTP, and so on.	REST data transfer occurs over HTTP only.
It is difficult to call a SOAP service from JavaScript.	It is very easy to call a REST service from JavaScript.

Single-page application model

Traditionally, in a web application, the client requests the server for a web page. Then, the server responds to the client with the requested HTML page after validating and authenticating the request, if necessary. The next request to the server might occur when a user hits some link on the page, submits a form, and so on. The server again processes the request and sends back the response with another HTML page.

Don't you think instead of getting the whole HTML page (which would be mostly the same look and feel as the last loaded page), we should just get the data we need and update the currently loaded page itself without posting back to the server? Yes, modern web development works in that regard. Today, we just need data from the server on demand using Ajax. After receiving the data, we will just update the UI with JavaScript or a client-side framework such as Angular.

This is what we call a **single-page application (SPA)**. On the first request to the server, the server responds with the entire page for the app. Unlike traditional web apps, subsequent requests won't ask for an HTML page, rather they will ask for data using Ajax requests where the type of content is usually JSON. After getting data, the browser has to update only the portion of the page that has changed instead of reloading the entire page again. The SPA definitely improves user experiences by responding quickly to user actions on the same page because reloading the page takes away a user's attention for a moment.

However, implementing SPA is not so easy as we have to be sure that we are showing fresh data on the page whenever needed. Here, emerging technologies, such as ASP.NET Web API, and JavaScript frameworks, such as AngularJS and CSS3 come in handy when designing SPAs.

Your application can call different endpoints of the REST API to do certain tasks and update the UI after getting responses without reloading the page.

Service-oriented architecture

Like SPA, Web API plays an important role in **service-oriented architecture (SOA)**. As the name suggests, it is an architecture methodology that deals with separation of responsibility from a business-oriented point of view into independent services. Often, these independent services or components can be designed using RESTful Web APIs.

Consider an e-commerce application that would have different components such as ordering, billing, payment processing, customer profile management, and so on. Each of these components has its own business logic and can be implemented independently.

The following diagram represents a pictorial view of such an application having independent components:

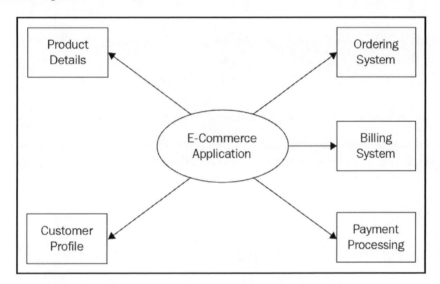

To make them independent, RESTful APIs can be exposed for these components, which can be easily consumed by any client/application including other components as well, as long as they satisfy the authentication and authorization.

Following is a pictorial representation of a monolithic or traditional application architecture versus SOA. It's perfectly clear how SOA introduces reusable components for the same business application. Moreover, implementing them with Web API brings the capability to expose that to outside for consumption by any application:

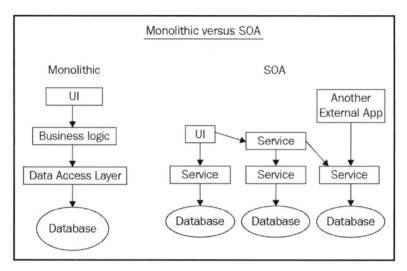

SOA implementation is beyond the scope of this book because there is a lot of stuff about Web API we need to explore in the next chapters. Whatever we do with the application in this book would use one Web API, but you can separate them out to build a more scalable architecture.

Summary

We started with some basic knowledge of SOAP and then we moved towards REST gradually.

This chapter shed some light on the fundamental REST building blocks and how they actually work. We explored the different status codes returned by widely used HTTP verbs.

To explore the request and response cycles of Web API, you can use Postman, where you not only have control over what is being sent and received, but also the ability to get code for different languages in order to consume the API.

ASP.NET Core attributes can be tied to controller action methods to make them more expressive and manageable in terms of routing and arguments.

Single-page applications can be easily designed using client-side technologies and consuming ASP.NET Core Web APIs so that pages can be updated as soon as responses are received to have a smooth user experience.

Web APIs can be plugged into the *service-oriented architecture* to have a modular design that improves scalability. By separating different critical components of the whole architecture with the help of APIs, it leaves us in a better position to reuse the components in different applications and expose them to the world so that they can be consumed by anyone.

In the next chapter, we will look at the important parts of the Web API architecture related to authentication.

3
User Registration and Administration

We built the foundation of the app in the last chapter, where we also explored the HTTP verbs in detail while creating a controller inside the ASP.NET Core Web API.

Now, we are gradually moving toward an important aspect of the API, called **authentication**. Authentication is definitely a required component because of the ease of accessibility of the API. Limiting the requests and putting a restriction on them would prevent malicious attacks.

Users of your application, or customers, in our case, need a registration form/interface where their details can be grabbed by the system. We will see how to register users with the API.

After you register and have all the details of the customers, such as *email* and *password*, it will be easy for you to identify the requests coming from a client. Wait, that is easy, but there are principles we need to follow in order to authenticate the user to access our resources. That is where *Basic Authentication* and *OAuth Authentication* will come into the picture.

We will cover the following topics in this chapter:

- Why authentication and limiting requests?
- Using EF Core for bootstrapping our REST API
- Adding basic authentication to our REST API
- Adding Oauth 2.0 authentication to our service
- Defining the client-based API consumption architecture

Why authentication and limiting requests?

If I told you that there is a Web API exposed from a particular country's government that you can use to get all the details of its citizens, then the first thing you would ask me is whether you can extract data from the API or not. That is exactly what we will be discussing.

So, if you take the previous example, the data that comes back from that API would have the citizens' sensitive data, such as *name, address, phone number, country, and social security number*. The government should never allow everyone to access this data. Only authenticated sources are allowed, generally. What that means is when you call one API, you need to send your identity and ask to it to allow you to operate on the data. If the identity is wrong or not in the list of allowed sources, it will be rejected by the API. Imagine terrorists trying to access the API, you would definitely deny access by detecting their identity.

Now imagine another scenario, where a university has an API that sends out results of a particular semester of a certain course. Many other websites would show the results on their site by calling this university API. A hacker comes in and uses a code block to call the API in a loop. If the time interval is too small, then don't be surprised if you get a **Server Busy/Server Unreachable** message. That is because, with a huge number of requests in a short span of time, the server becomes overloaded and runs out of resources.

That is where imposing limitations on the API not to allow more requests from the same source in a particular time interval comes into the picture. For example, if any consumer accesses our API, we will not allow the request if the consumer has already requested it before in the last 10 seconds or so.

First, let's design the database for our app before exploring other concepts.

Database design

We will definitely have a *Customers* table. We will store customer information in that table and use the primary key of this table as a reference in other tables, such as *Orders* and *Cart*.

The **Customers** table can be designed as follows. You can find the database script, named `FlixOneStore.sql`, with this book:

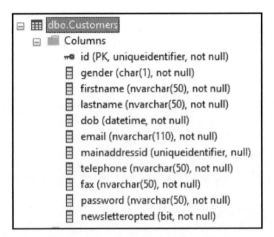

CRUD operations will be performed on these tables from the API. Let's start by doing some operations on this table from the API. More precisely, we are talking about the customer registration and login process.

User registration

Let's get the models into the API first so that we can create an object and save data in the database. We will use **Entity Framework Core (EF Core)** version 2.0.2 for this.

Setting up EF with the API

To use EF Core, the following package is required, which can be downloaded and installed from **NuGet Package Manager** inside **Tools**:

Additionally, we need another package named **Microsoft.EntityFrameworkCore.Tools**. This will help us with creating model classes from the database:

.NET **Microsoft.EntityFrameworkCore.Tools** ⊘ by Microsoft, **3.88M** downloads v2.0.2

Entity Framework Core Package Manager Console Tools. Includes Scaffold-DbContext, Add-Migration, and Update-Database.

Now, we arrive at the point where we need model classes according to the database tables. The following powershell command can be executed inside the package manager console to create the model class for the *Customers* table:

```
Scaffold-DbContext
"Server=.;Database=FlixOneStore;Trusted_Connection=True;"
Microsoft.EntityFrameworkCore.SqlServer -OutputDir Models -Tables Customers
```

We have provided the connection string in the command so that it connects to our database.

The following are two important parts of the command we just explored:

- `-OutputDir Models`: This defines the folder in which the model class will be placed.
- `-Tables Customers`: This defines the table that will be extracted as the model class. We will be dealing with *Customers* for now.

After execution, you will see two files, `Customers.cs` and `FixOneStoreContext.cs`, inside the `Models` folder. The `Customers.cs` file will be something like the following:

```csharp
using System;
namespace DemoECommerceApp.Models
{
  public partial class Customers
  {
    public Guid Id { get; set; }
    public string Gender { get; set; }
    public string Firstname { get; set; }
    public string Lastname { get; set; }
    public DateTime Dob { get; set; }
    public string Email { get; set; }
    public Guid? Mainaddressid { get; set; }
    public string Telephone { get; set; }
    public string Fax { get; set; }
```

```
    public string Password { get; set; }
    public bool Newsletteropted { get; set; }
  }
}
```

Configuring DbContext

The context class can be found in the same folder that has the OnConfiguring and OnModelCreating methods with a property for *Customers*.

The following code block shows the FlixOneStoreContext class:

```
using Microsoft.EntityFrameworkCore;
namespace DemoECommerceApp.Models
{
  public partial class FlixOneStoreContext : DbContext
  {
    public virtual DbSet<Customers> Customers { get; set; }
    public FlixOneStoreContext(DbContextOptions<
    FlixOneStoreContext> options)
    : base(options)
    { }
    // Code is commented below, because we are applying
    dependency injection inside startup.
    // protected override void OnConfiguring(
    DbContextOptionsBuilder optionsBuilder)
    // {
    // if (!optionsBuilder.IsConfigured)
    // {
    //#warning To protect potentially sensitive information
    in your connection string, you should move it out of
    source code. See http://go.microsoft.com/fwlink/?LinkId=723263
    for guidance on storing connection strings.
    // optionsBuilder.UseSqlServer(@"Server=.;
    Database=FlixOneStore;Trusted_Connection=True;");
    // }
    // }
    protected override void OnModelCreating(ModelBuilder modelBuilder)
    {
      modelBuilder.Entity<Customers>(entity =>
      {
        entity.Property(e => e.Id)
        .HasColumnName("id")
        .ValueGeneratedNever();
        entity.Property(e => e.Dob)
        .HasColumnName("dob")
```

```
                .HasColumnType("datetime");
                entity.Property(e => e.Email)
                .IsRequired()
                .HasColumnName("email")
                .HasMaxLength(110);
                entity.Property(e => e.Fax)
                .IsRequired()
                .HasColumnName("fax")
                .HasMaxLength(50);
                entity.Property(e => e.Firstname)
                .IsRequired()
                .HasColumnName("firstname")
                .HasMaxLength(50);
                entity.Property(e => e.Gender)
                .IsRequired()
                .HasColumnName("gender")
                .HasColumnType("char(1)");
                entity.Property(e => e.Lastname)
                .IsRequired()
                .HasColumnName("lastname")
                .HasMaxLength(50);
                entity.Property(e => e.Mainaddressid).HasColumnName
                ("mainaddressid");
                entity.Property(e => e.Newsletteropted).HasColumnName
                ("newsletteropted");
                entity.Property(e => e.Password)
                .IsRequired()
                .HasColumnName("password")
                .HasMaxLength(50);
                entity.Property(e => e.Telephone)
                .IsRequired()
                .HasColumnName("telephone")
                .HasMaxLength(50);
            });
        }
    }
}
```

Did you notice that I have commented the OnConfiguring method and added a constructor so that we can inject dependencies from startup to initialize the context with a connection string? Let's do that.

So, inside the `ConfigureServices` startup, we will add the context to the services collection using the connection string:

```
public void ConfigureServices(IServiceCollection services)
{
    services.AddSingleton<IProductService, ProductService>();
    services.AddMvc();
    var connection = @"Server=.;Database=FlixOneStore;
    Trusted_Connection=True";
    services.AddDbContext<FlixOneStoreContext>(
    options => options.UseSqlServer(connection));
}
```

Generating the controller

The next step is to add the controller. To do so, refer to the following steps:

1. Right-click on the `Controller` folder, then click on **Add**, followed by **Controller**. You will end up on a modal where you will see options to create different types of controllers:

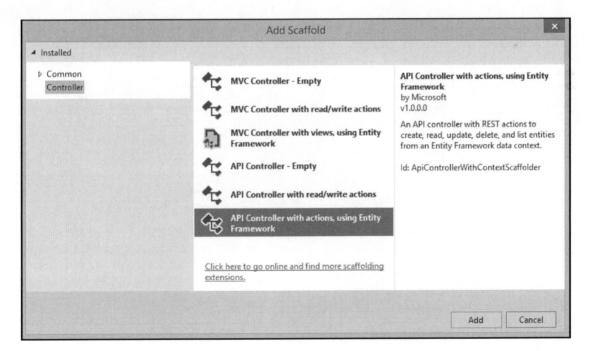

2. Select **API Controller with actions, using Entity Framework** and click on the **Add** button. The following screenshot shows what happens next:

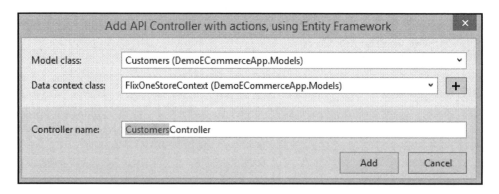

3. Click on **Add**. *Voila!* It did all that hard work and created a fully fledged controller using EF Core with actions using all major HTTP verbs. The following code block is a small snapshot of the controller with the GET methods only. I have removed other methods to save space:

```csharp
// Removed usings for brevity.
namespace DemoECommerceApp.Controllers
{
    [Produces("application/json")]
    [Route("api/Customers")]
    public class CustomersController : Controller
    {
        private readonly FlixOneStoreContext _context;
        public CustomersController(FlixOneStoreContext context)
        {
            _context = context;
        }
        // GET: api/Customers
        [HttpGet]
        public IEnumerable<Customers> GetCustomers()
        {
            return _context.Customers;
        }
        // GET: api/Customers/5
        [HttpGet("{id}")]
        public async Task<IActionResult> GetCustomers
        ([FromRoute] Guid id)
        {
            if (!ModelState.IsValid)
            {
```

```
        return BadRequest(ModelState);
    }
    var customers = await
    _context.Customers.SingleOrDefaultAsync(m => m.Id == id);
    if (customers == null)
    {
        return NotFound();
    }
    return Ok(customers);
}

// You will also find PUT POST, DELETE methods.
// These action methods are removed to save space.
    }
}
```

Some points to note here:

- Notice how FlixOneStoreContext is initialized here by injecting it into the constructor. Further more, it will be used for database-related operations inside all actions:

```
private readonly FlixOneStoreContext _context;
public CustomersController(FlixOneStoreContext context)
{
    _context = context;
}
```

- The next thing to focus on is the methods used to return the results from the actions. See how BadRequest(), NotFound(), Ok(), and NoContent() are used to return proper HTTP response codes that can be easily understood by clients. We will see what codes they return in a while when we call these actions to perform real tasks.

Calling the API from a page to register the customer

To simplify things, I have designed a simple HTML page with controls for a customer record, as follows. We will input data and try to call the API in order to save the record:

```
<div class="container">
  <h2>Register for FlixOneStore</h2>
  <div class="form-horizontal">
    <div class="form-group">
```

```
      <label class="control-label col-sm-2" for=
      "txtFirstName">First Name:</label>
      <div class="col-sm-3">
        <input type="text" class="form-control" id=
        "txtFirstName" placeholder=
        "Enter first name" name="firstname">
      </div>
  </div>
  <div class="form-group">
      <label class="control-label col-sm-2" for=
      "txtLastName">Last Name:</label>
      <div class="col-sm-3">
        <input type="text" class="form-control" id=
        "txtLastName" placeholder=
        "Enter last name" name="lastname">
      </div>
  </div>
  <div class="form-group">
      <label class="control-label col-sm-2" for="txtEmail">
      Email:</label>
      <div class="col-sm-3">
        <input type="email" class="form-control" id=
        "txtEmail" placeholder=
        "Enter email" name="email">
      </div>
  </div>
  <div class="form-group">
      <label class="control-label col-sm-2" for="gender">
      Gender:</label>
      <div class="col-sm-3">
        <label class="radio-inline"><input type="radio"
        value="M" name="gender">Male</label>
        <lable class="radio-inline"><input type="radio"
        value="F" name="gender">Female</lable>
      </div>
  </div>
  <div class="form-group">
      <label class="control-label col-sm-2" for="txtDob">
      Date of Birth:</label>
      <div class="col-sm-3">
        <input type="date" class="form-control" id="txtDob" />
      </div>
  </div>
  <div class="form-group">
      <label class="control-label col-sm-2" for="txtMobile">
      Mobile Number:</label>
      <div class="col-sm-3">
        <input type="text" class="form-control" id="txtMobile"
```

```
        placeholder=
        "Enter mobile number" />
      </div>
    </div>
    <div class="form-group">
      <label class="control-label col-sm-2" for="txtFax">Fax:</label>
      <div class="col-sm-3">
        <input type="text" class="form-control" id="txtFax"
        placeholder="Enter fax" />
      </div>
    </div>
    <div class="form-group">
      <label class="control-label col-sm-2" for="txtPassword">
      Password:</label>
      <div class="col-sm-3">
        <input type="password" class="form-control" id=
        "txtPassword" placeholder=
        "Enter password" name="pwd">
      </div>
    </div>
    <div class="form-group">
      <label class="control-label col-sm-2" for="txtConfirmPassword">
      Confirm Password:</label>
      <div class="col-sm-3">
        <input type="password" class="form-control"
        id="txtConfirmPassword" placeholder=
        "Enter password again" name="confirmpwd">
      </div>
    </div>
    <div class="form-group">
      <div class="col-sm-offset-2 col-sm-10">
        <button type="button" class="btn btn-success"
        id="btnRegister">Register</button>
      </div>
    </div>
  </div>
</div>
```

I have used bootstrap and *jQuery* with my code. You can refer to the whole code in the attached files with the book or refer to `https://github.com/PacktPublishing/Building-RESTful-Web-services-with-DOTNET-Core`.

Now comes the important part of the code, where we will call the API to store the customer record. Refer to the following code block:

```
$(document).ready(function () {
    $('#btnRegister').click(function () {
```

```
// Check password and confirm password.
var password = $('#txtPassword').val(),
confirmPassword = $('#txtConfirmPassword').val();
if (password !== confirmPassword) {
  alert("Password and Confirm Password don't match!");
  return;
}

// Make a customer object.
var customer = {
  "gender": $("input[name='gender']:checked").val(),
  "firstname": $('#txtFirstName').val(),
  "lastname": $('#txtLastName').val(),
  "dob": $('#txtDob').val(),
  "email": $('#txtEmail').val(),
  "telephone": $('#txtMobile').val(),
  "fax": $('#txtFax').val(),
  "password": $('#txtPassword').val(),
  "newsletteropted": false
};

$.ajax({
  url: 'http://localhost:57571/api/Customers',
  type: "POST",
  contentType: "application/json",
  data: JSON.stringify(customer),
  dataType: "json",
  success: function (result) {
    alert("A customer record created for: "
    + result.firstname + " " + result.lastname);
  },
  error: function (err) {
    alert(err.responseText);
  }
});
});
});
```

Notice the `http://localhost:57571/api/Customers` URL and POST HTTP method. This eventually calls the `Post` method present in the API named `PostCustomers`. We will definitely have some uniqueness in the table, and in our case, I am taking email as unique for each record. That's why I need to modify the `action` method a little bit:

```
// POST: api/Customers
[HttpPost]
public async Task<IActionResult> PostCustomers([FromBody] Customers
customers)
```

```
{
  if (!ModelState.IsValid)
  {
    return BadRequest(ModelState);
  }
  // Unique mail id check.
  if (_context.Customers.Any(x => x.Email == customers.Email))
  {
    ModelState.AddModelError("email", "User with mail id already
    exists!");
    return BadRequest(ModelState);
  }
  _context.Customers.Add(customers);
  try
  {
    await _context.SaveChangesAsync();
  }
  catch (DbUpdateException ex)
  {
    if (CustomersExists(customers.Id))
    {
      return new StatusCodeResult(StatusCodes.Status409Conflict);
    }
    else
    {
      throw;
    }
  }
  return CreatedAtAction("GetCustomers", new { id = customers.Id },
  customers);
}
```

I am returning `BadRequest()` by adding an error message for the model property email. We will see how this is shown on the browser shortly!

The following image captured from the browser shows you a successful *customer* creation:

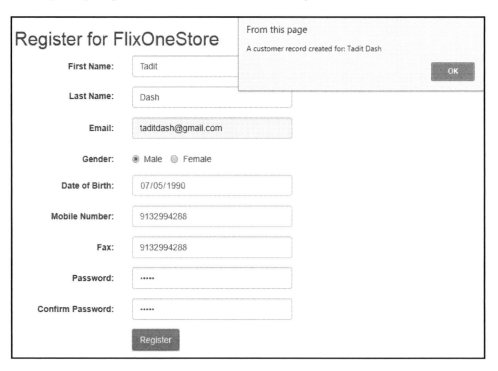

A successful registration of a *customer* would look something like the preceding image, which shows us the success message in the alert as we have that inside the `success` method of the ajax call.

You can perform anything you want with the data received from the `action` method upon completion, as it returns the whole `customer` object. If you don't believe me, refer to the following screenshot from the source window of the debugger tool:

```
$.ajax({
    url: 'http://localhost:57571/api/Customers',
    type: "POST",
    contentType: "application/json",
    data: JSON.stringify(customer),
    dataType: "json",
    success: function (result) {   result = {id: "910d4c2f-b394-4578-
        alert("A custo
            + result.    Object
    },                   dob: "1990-07-05T00:00:00"
    error: function (    email: "taditdash@gmail.com"
        alert(err.res    fax: "9132994288"
    }                    firstname: "Tadit"
});                      gender: "M"
                         id: "910d4c2f-b394-4578-8d9c-7ca3fd3266e2"
                         lastname: "Dash"
                         mainaddressid: null
                         newsletteropted: false
"container">             password: "12345"
ister for FlixOneStore   telephone: "9132994288"
                       ▶ __proto__: Object
5
```

The response to the POST request with the new Customer created inside the jQuery Ajax success method

So, who did this? Simple, the following return statement, which is inside the POST method, does all the magic:

```
return CreatedAtAction("GetCustomers", new { id = customers.Id },
customers);
```

This particular line does a couple of things:

- Sends **Status Code: 201 Created** as the POST action successfully created the resource.
- Sets a **Location** header with the actual URL for the resource. If you remember RESTful characteristics, after the POST action, the server should send the URL of the resource. That is what it does.

Let me show you the network tab of developer tools to prove my point. You can also use *Postman* and analyze it. The following screenshot shows you the response details:

```
▼ General
    Request URL: http://localhost:57571/api/Customers
    Request Method: POST
    Status Code: ● 201 Created
    Remote Address: [::1]:57571
    Referrer Policy: no-referrer-when-downgrade
▼ Response Headers      view source
    Access-Control-Allow-Origin: *
    Content-Type: application/json; charset=utf-8
    Date: Tue, 01 May 2018 02:54:02 GMT
    Location: http://localhost:57571/api/Customers/3cd92f52-323d-43ca-a26b-0b13576612d9
    Server: Kestrel
    Transfer-Encoding: chunked
    X-Powered-By: ASP.NET
```

The response received by a POST success request with Status Code and Location Header

`Guid` is actually the `Customer ID` as we have defined it in the column type in database, and I am assigning the value to it inside the `Customer` model class constructor.

Now, if you copy this URL and open it in your browser or Postman, you will get the details of the customer, as the following screenshot shows you:

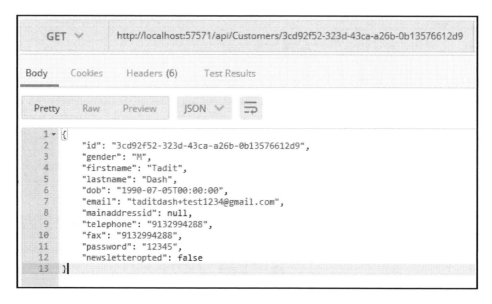

Let's see a `BadRequest()` example with a mail ID that already exists. As the `taditdash@gmail.com` customer already exists, sending another request with the same email ID should send us an error message as a response. Let's have a look:

Remember, we added a line to check the email ID existence and added a `ModelState` error. That is in action now.

 For simplicity of the demo in this book, I am just saving a plain text password. You should not do that in the actual project. Implementing proper encryption for a password is a must.

With this, I would end the registration process. However, there is scope to implement validation at the client side as well as at the server side. You can add attributes to the `Model` class properties to make it solid so that you don't get bad data from clients. Send a `BadRequest()` response when `ModelState` validation fails. Required email-format and password-comparison attributes can be added to the `Model` class.

CORS

If you see the following error when you call the API action, then you need to enable **Cross Origin Resource Sharing (CORS)**:

```
Failed to load http://localhost:57571/api/Customers: Response to preflight
request doesn't pass access control check: No 'Access-Control-Allow-Origin'
header is present on the requested resource. Origin 'null' is therefore not
allowed access. The response had HTTP status code 404.
```

To enable CORS for all origins, follow the steps shown ahead:

1. Install the `Microsoft.AspNetCore.Cors` NuGet package:

 Microsoft.AspNetCore.Cors ⊘ by Microsoft, 7.64M downloads
CORS middleware and policy for ASP.NET Core to enable cross-origin resource sharing.
Commonly used types:

2. Inside `Startup ConfigureServices`, add the following code to implement a policy for CORS that would allow all origins:

```
services.AddCors(options =>
{
  options.AddPolicy("AllowAll",
    builder =>
    {
      builder
      .AllowAnyOrigin()
      .AllowAnyMethod()
      .AllowAnyHeader();
    });
});
```

3. Inside the `Configure` method, add the following line before `app.UseMvc();` (it's important):

```
app.UseCors("AllowAll");
```

Now, it should work as expected. If you want to explore CORS more, visit `https://docs.microsoft.com/en-us/aspnet/core/security/cors?view=aspnetcore-2.1`.

Adding basic authentication to our REST API

Now that we registered the *customer*, we can move towards the authentication process. Authentication is to verify whether a *customer* is a valid user of our site or not. We already have their credentials with us since they registered using our registration form. When they try to access any resource from our site using those credentials, we will verify first and then allow.

Registration will be allowed for everyone and won't be authenticated. However, when a *customer* wants to *read their profile details* or *delete their account,* and so on, then we need authentication in place so that the data is returned to users who are actual trusted users of the application.

For *basic authentication*:

- We will get the *username*, which will be the *email ID* and *password* from the client while they request a resource. This will be sent with HTTP headers. We will see it when we design the client.
- Then, that data will be verified from the database.
- If found, the operation will be allowed, otherwise a `401 Unauthorized` response will be sent.

Step 1 – Adding the (authorize) attribute

Let's restrict the action method that is returning the *customer* profile details, the `GET` method of `CustomersController` named `GetCustomers([FromRoute] Guid id)`.

We will verify the following two things when a *customer* is trying to access the profile:

- The request is coming from a trusted user of the application. Meaning, the request is coming from a *customer* having a valid *email* and *password*.
- The customer can only access their profile. To check this, we will verify the *customer's* credentials (present in the request) with the requested *customer's* ID on the URL.

Let's get started. Remember that our goal is to achieve the following:

```
[Authorize(AuthenticationSchemes = "Basic")]
public async Task<IActionResult> GetCustomers([FromRoute] Guid id)
```

For now, we will focus our attention on this action method to understand the concept. You can see the `Authorize` attribute with an `AuthenticationScheme` defined as `Basic` here. That means we have to tell the runtime what the *basic authentication* is so that it will execute that first before going into the action method.

If the authentication succeeds, the action method will be executed, otherwise a **401 Unauthorized response** will be sent to the client.

Step 2 – Designing BasicAuthenticationOptions and BasicAuthenticationHandler

First of all, we need a class that would derive the `AuthenticationSchemeOptions` class present in `Microsoft.AspNetCore.Authentication`, as shown in the following code block:

```
using Microsoft.AspNetCore.Authentication;
namespace DemoECommerceApp.Security.Authentication
{
    public class BasicAuthenticationOptions : AuthenticationSchemeOptions {}
}
```

It is left blank for simplicity but can be loaded with different properties. We will not go into that.

Next, we need a handler for *basic authentication*, where we will have our actual logic:

```
public class BasicAuthenticationHandler :
AuthenticationHandler<BasicAuthenticationOptions>
```

We can have its constructor-like following with an extra `DbContext` param as we will validate the *customer* details from the database:

```
public
BasicAuthenticationHandler(IOptionsMonitor<BasicAuthenticationOptions>
options, ILoggerFactory logger, UrlEncoder encoder, ISystemClock clock,
FlixOneStoreContext context)
: base(options, logger, encoder, clock)
```

```
{
    _context = context;
}
```

AuthenticationHandler<T> is an abstract class having properties and methods related to authentication especially. We will be overriding two methods, for now, HandleAuthenticateAsync and HandleChallengeAsync. HandleAuthenticateAsync will have actual logic to authenticate the customer and HandleChallengeAsync is used to deal with 401 challenge concerns, meaning whenever you decide that *customer* is not valid, codes can be written in this method to deal with that situation.

We are assuming that we will receive the email and password in the HTTP header called Authorization separated by a delimiter colon (:). The following is the code to extract the data from the header and validate whether it is correct or not:

```
protected override Task<AuthenticateResult> HandleAuthenticateAsync()
{
    // 1. Verify if AuthorizationHeaderName present in the header.
    // AuthorizationHeaderName is a string with value "Authorization".
    if (!Request.Headers.ContainsKey(AuthorizationHeaderName))
    {
        // Authorization header not found.
        return Task.FromResult(AuthenticateResult.NoResult());
    }
    // 2. Verify if header is valid.
    if (!AuthenticationHeaderValue.TryParse(Request.Headers
    [AuthorizationHeaderName], out AuthenticationHeaderValue
    headerValue))
    {
        // Authorization header is not valid.
        return Task.FromResult(AuthenticateResult.NoResult());
    }
    // 3. Verify is scheme name is Basic. BasicSchemeName is a string
    // with value 'Basic'.
    if (!BasicSchemeName.Equals(headerValue.Scheme, StringComparison.
    OrdinalIgnoreCase))
    {
        // Authorization header is not Basic.
        return Task.FromResult(AuthenticateResult.NoResult());
    }
    // 4. Fetch email and password from header.
    // If length is not 2, then authentication fails.
    byte[] headerValueBytes = Convert.FromBase64String(headerValue.
    Parameter);
    string emailPassword = Encoding.UTF8.GetString(headerValueBytes);
    string[] parts = emailPassword.Split(':');
```

```
if (parts.Length != 2)
{
  return Task.FromResult(AuthenticateResult.Fail("Invalid Basic
  Authentication Header"));
}
string email = parts[0];
string password = parts[1];
// 5. Validate if email and password are correct.
var customer = _context.Customers.SingleOrDefault(x =>
x.Email == email && x.Password == password);
if (customer == null)
{
  return Task.FromResult(AuthenticateResult.Fail("Invalid email
  and password."));
}
// 6. Create claims with email and id.
var claims = new[]
{
  new Claim(ClaimTypes.Name, email),
  new Claim(ClaimTypes.NameIdentifier, customer.Id.ToString())
};
// 7. ClaimsIdentity creation with claims.
var identity = new ClaimsIdentity(claims, Scheme.Name);
var principal = new ClaimsPrincipal(identity);
var ticket = new AuthenticationTicket(principal, Scheme.Name);
return Task.FromResult(AuthenticateResult.Success(ticket));
}
```

The code is very easy to understand. I have added the steps over code blocks. Basically, we are trying to validate the header and then process it to see whether they are correct. If correct, then create the ClaimsIdentity object, which can be further used in the application. We will do that in the next section. At each step, if validation fails, we send AuthenticateResult.NoResult() or AuthenticateResult.Fail().

Let's work on attaching this authentication to our action method, using something like the following:

```
[HttpGet("{id}")]
[Authorize(AuthenticationSchemes = "Basic")]
public async Task<IActionResult> GetCustomers([FromRoute] Guid id)
{
  if (!ModelState.IsValid)
  {
    return BadRequest(ModelState);
  }
  var ident = User.Identity as ClaimsIdentity;
  var currentLoggeedInUserId = ident.Claims.FirstOrDefault
```

```
(c => c.Type == ClaimTypes.NameIdentifier)?.Value;
if (currentLoggeedInUserId != id.ToString())
{
   // Not Authorized
   return BadRequest("You are not authorized!");
}
var customers = await _context.Customers.SingleOrDefaultAsync
(m => m.Id == id);
if (customers == null)
{
   return NotFound();
}
return Ok(customers);
}
```

Step 3 – Registering basic authentication at startup

Looks like everything is set up, however, we have missed one step of registering this basic authentication in the startup. Otherwise, how could the `BasicAuthenticationHandler` handler be called? Have a look:

```
services.AddAuthentication("Basic")
.AddScheme<BasicAuthenticationOptions, BasicAuthenticationHandler>("Basic",
null);
services.AddTransient<IAuthenticationHandler,
BasicAuthenticationHandler>();
```

To test the API, you can design an HTML page to show the profile of the user by getting details from the API using the `Id`. You can use the *jQuery Ajax* call to the API and operate on the result received:

```
$.ajax({
   url: 'http://localhost:57571/api/Customers/
   910D4C2F-B394-4578-8D9C-7CA3FD3266E2',
   type: "GET",
   contentType: "application/json",
   dataType: "json",
   headers: { 'Authorization': 'Basic ' + btoa
   (email + ':' + password)},
   success: function (result) {
      // Work with result. Code removed for brevity.
   },
   error: function (err)
```

```
  {
    if (err.status == 401)
    {
      alert("Either wrong email and password or you are
      not authorized to access the data!")
    }
  }
});
```

Notice the header part where we have the `Authorization` header mentioned with `email` and `password` separated by a colon (`:`) and passed to the `btoa` method, which is responsible for Base64 encryption. After you get the result, you can do *n* number of things. The following screenshot shows it on the page using some bootstrap designing:

Now, there is an important code block that should be included with the previous handler code. That is another `HandleChallengeAsync` method that should be overridden. The purpose of this method is to handle the situation when the authentication fails.

We will just send one header with the response, named `WWW-Authenticate`, whose value can be set with a `realm`. Have a look at the code first and then I will explain:

```
protected override async Task HandleChallengeAsync(AuthenticationProperties
properties)
{
  Response.Headers["WWW-Authenticate"] = $"Basic
  realm=\"http://localhost:57571\", charset=\"UTF-8\"";
  await base.HandleChallengeAsync(properties);
}
```

 If a client tries to access a restricted resource or a resource that requires authentication, it's the server's responsibility to inform the client about the authentication type and related information. The `WWW-Authenticate` HTTP response header is set by the server that defines the authentication method that should be used to gain access to the restricted resource requested.

So, it's obvious that the `WWW-Authenticate` header is sent along with a **401 Unauthorized** response. The string contains three things: *Authentication Type*, *Realm*, and *Charset*. The realm is the domain or area where the authentication will be valid.

In our case, the scheme is `Basic`, Realm is `http://localhost:57571`, and Charset is `UTF-8`. Therefore, if the client provides the basic authentication params as `Username` and `Password`, those will be valid in the `localhost:57571` domain.

That is what it signifies. So, just remove the header assigning a code or comment it out to test this. The following is the screenshot from the **Network** tab of the developer tool in Chrome:

Have a look at the following screenshot of an alert message, which we have inside the error method of the Ajax call. This happens when the API action is called without any credentials:

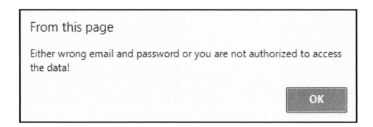

Adding OAuth 2.0 authentication to our service

OAuth is an open standard used by APIs to control access to the resources by clients, such as websites, desktop applications, or even other APIs. However, the API implementing OAuth can provide user information without sharing the password with third-party apps.

You must have seen websites where they allow logins using different services, such as Facebook, Twitter, or Google, saying something such as (for Facebook) **Login with Facebook**. That means Facebook has an OAuth server that would validate your app by a certain identity that you have provided to Facebook earlier, and give you an access token that would have some validity. Using that token, you can read the required user's profile.

The following is some basic OAuth2.0 terminology:

- **Resource:** We have already defined this in previous chapters. Resources are the things that we need to protect. That may be any information related to our system.
- **Resource server:** This is the server that would protect the resource, mostly the API that we have designed to access our eCommerce database.
- **Resource owner:** The person who would grant us access to a particular resource. Mostly the users are the owners, and as you have seen when you click on **Login with Facebook**, it will ask for your login and consent.
- **Client:** The app that wants our resource access. In our case, it is the browser that is trying to access the resources when *jQuery* codes are executed on the HTML pages we designed.
- **Access token:** This is actually the pillar of this architecture. The OAuth server that we will design should provide a token using the credentials of the user for subsequent access to our resources, as we know OAuth standard tells us not provide passwords to clients.
- **Bearer token:** This is a particular type of access token that allows anyone to use the token easily, meaning, in order to use the token for resource access, a client doesn't need a cryptographic key or other secret keys. As this is less secure than other types of tokens, bearer tokens should only be used over HTTPs and should expire in a short amount of time.
- **Authorization server:** This is the server providing the access token to the client.

Let's start adding OAuth to our Web API. We are going to use **IdentityServer4**, which is a free, open source OpenID Connect and OAuth 2.0 framework for ASP.NET Core. The project can be found here: `https://github.com/IdentityServer`.

IdentityServer (`http://identityserver.io/`) is based on OWIN/Katana, but to our knowledge, it is distributed and available as a NuGet package. In order to start on IdentityServer, install the following two NuGet Packages:

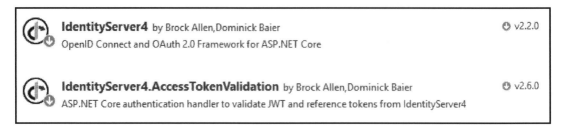

IdentityServer4 by Brock Allen, Dominick Baier   v2.2.0
OpenID Connect and OAuth 2.0 Framework for ASP.NET Core

IdentityServer4.AccessTokenValidation by Brock Allen, Dominick Baier   v2.6.0
ASP.NET Core authentication handler to validate JWT and reference tokens from IdentityServer4

The *authorization server* in a production scenario is ideally isolated from the main web API. But for this book, we will directly put that in the same Web API project for simplicity. We are not using the default ASP.NET Core Identity. We will be using our own set of tables. For instance, we will use our *customer* table details for verification.

Step 1 – Designing the Config class

The `Config` class holds important details of the authorization server, such as *Resources*, *Clients*, and *Users*. These details are used while generating the token. Let's design it:

```
public class Config
{
  public static IEnumerable<ApiResource> GetApiResources()
  {
    return new List<ApiResource>
    {
      new ApiResource
      (
        "FlixOneStore.ReadAccess",
        "FlixOneStore API",
        new List<string>
        {
          JwtClaimTypes.Id,
          JwtClaimTypes.Email,
          JwtClaimTypes.Name,
          JwtClaimTypes.GivenName,
          JwtClaimTypes.FamilyName
        }
      ),
```

```
        new ApiResource("FlixOneStore.FullAccess", "FlixOneStore API")
    };
  }
}
```

`ApiResource` is used to declare different scopes and claims for the API. For a simple case, an API might have one simple resource structure where it would give access to all clients. However, in a typical scenario, clients can be restricted to access different parts of the API. While declaring the clients, we will use these resources in order to configure their scope and access rights. `ReadAccess` and `FullAccess` are two different resource types that can be used with clients to give read and full access, respectively.

Basically, the methods that we are designing now will be called on `Startup`. Here, `GetApiResources` is actually creating two types of resource with different settings. The first one is what we will be dealing with for the moment. We have named it `FlixOneStore.ReadAccess`. You can see a list of strings with `Id`, `Name`, and so on, these are the details of the customer that will be generated with the token and passed to the client.

Let's add details for a client from where we will consume the authorization server:

```
public static IEnumerable<Client> GetClients()
{
  return new[]
  {
    new Client
    {
      Enabled = true,
      ClientName = "HTML Page Client",
      ClientId = "htmlClient",
      AllowedGrantTypes = GrantTypes.ResourceOwnerPassword,

      ClientSecrets =
      {
        new Secret("secretpassword".Sha256())
      },

      AllowedScopes = { "FlixOneStore.ReadAccess" }
    }
  };
}
```

You can add a number of clients as per your needs. You can set *client id*, *client secret*, and *grant types* according to OAuth standards in this method. Notice the secret password is set as `secretpassword`. You can set any string here; it can be a `Guid`. Here, `GrantType.ResourceOwnerPassword` defines the way we will validate the incoming request to generate tokens.

It says to the *Authorization Server*, "Hey look for `username` and `password` inside the request body." There are other types of Grant available. You can explore more on the official documentation link.

You might have a question now! What are we going to do with `username` and `password`? Of course, we will validate them, but with what? The answer is the `Email` and `Password` fields from the `Customers` table. We have not done anything related to connecting *Authorization Server* with the *Customers* table. That is what we will do next. But before that, let's register these settings at `Startup`.

 Just to make sure we are on the same page, we landed at the point where we are trying to generate a token from the Authorization Server in order to access our API.

Step 2 – Registering Config at startup

For registration, the following is what we have to do inside the `ConfigureServices` method:

```
services.AddIdentityServer()
        .AddInMemoryApiResources(Config.GetApiResources())
        .AddInMemoryClients(Config.GetClients())
        .AddProfileService<ProfileService>()
        .AddDeveloperSigningCredential();
```

We are loading all those config settings here, such as *Resources* and *Clients*, by calling the methods we designed. `AddDeveloperSigningCredential` adds a temporary key at the startup time, used only on the development environment when we don't have any certificate to apply for Authorization. You would add proper certificate details for actual use.

Mark `ProfileService` here. This is what I was talking about in the previous section, which will be used to validate the user credentials against the database. We will look at it in a little while. First, let's test our API, assuming that the Authorization Server is ready with `ProfileService` set up.

Now coming to the API, we need to add `AuthenticationScheme` at the start of the API to declare what Authentication we will be using. For that, add the following code:

```
services.AddAuthentication(options =>
{
  options.DefaultAuthenticateScheme =
  JwtBearerDefaults.AuthenticationScheme;
  options.DefaultChallengeScheme =
  JwtBearerDefaults.AuthenticationScheme;
})
.AddJwtBearer(o =>
{
  o.Authority = "http://localhost:57571";
  o.Audience = "FlixOneStore.ReadAccess";
  o.RequireHttpsMetadata = false;
});
```

`JwtBearerDefaults.AuthenticationScheme` is actually a string constant with the **Bearer** value. **Bearer authentication** is also known as **token authentication**. That means our clients need to send a token in order to access the API's resources. And to get the token, they need to call our *authorization server*, available at `/connect/token`.

Notice we have `Audience` set as `FlixOneStore.ReadAccess`, which we have specified for the clients inside config. Simply put, we are setting up the bearer type of authentication.

Step 3 – Adding the [Authorize] attribute

The next thing is to add the `[Authorize]` attribute to the API controller action. Let's test this with the `GetCustomers(id)` method:

```
// GET: api/Customers/5
[HttpGet("{id}")]
[Authorize]
public async Task<IActionResult> GetCustomers([FromRoute] Guid id)
```

Calling it from the *Postman* yields the following output:

So, our request is not authorized anymore. We got a reply that we need to send a token in order to access the resource. Let's get the token, then.

Step 4 – Getting the token

In order to get the token, we need to call the authorization server sitting at `/connect/token`.

The following is a screen captured from *Postman* where a POST request is performed on the `http://localhost:57571/connect/token` URL with a body containing all the required parameters in order to authenticate the client. These are the details that we registered inside the `GetClients()` method in *Step 1*:

Oops! It's a bad request. That is because we passed the wrong secret password for the client. If you remember, we set it as `secretpassword`, but passed it as `secret`. That's why it got rejected.

Some important things to note here. To get the token:

- We need to send a `POST` request to the `/connect/token` URL. As we have implemented the server in the same app, the domain is the same here as the API.
- We need to have a `Content-Type` header set as `application/x-www-form-urlencoded` (which is actually in a different tab on the screenshot).
- In the body of the request, we added all the required parameters of OAuth according to standards and they match exactly what we had in the configuration class.

When we send everything as required correctly, we will receive a token, as shown in the following screenshot:

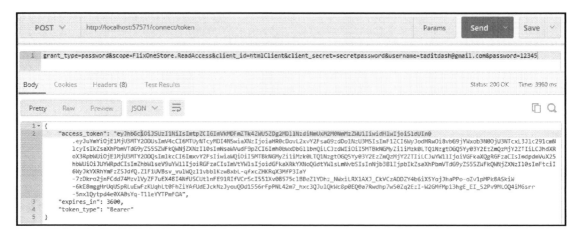

We received the bearer token response according to OAuth specifications. They are `access_token`, `expires_in`, and `token_type`. The `expires_in` param is set to 3,600 by default for the access token, which is in seconds, meaning 1 hour. After 1 hour, this token won't work anymore. Therefore, before this token expires, let's quickly call our API with it and see whether that works.

Step 5 – Calling the API with the access token

Have a look at the following picture, which shows you the call to the API using the token we just received:

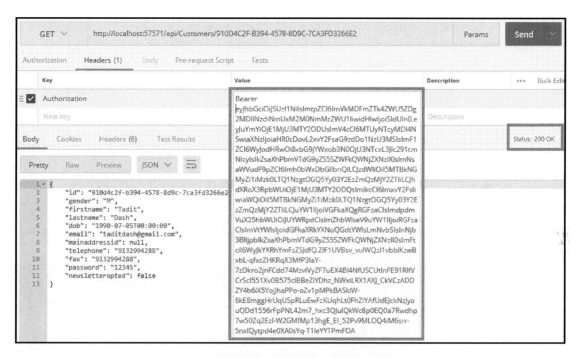

Calling the API endpoint with the token in the authorization header

Voila! That worked. I just copied the token I got and added in the `Bearer [Access Token]` format to the authorization header and sent the request. Everything is perfect now.

Step 6 – Adding the ProfileService class

While we explored all this, I left out one part that I want to explain now. If you see the body of the request while we fetch the access token, it is something like:

```
grant_type=password&scope=FlixOneStore.ReadAccess&client_id=htmlClient&clie
nt_secret=secretpassword&username=taditdash@gmail.com&password=12345
```

Focus on the `username` and `password` parameters. They are here for a reason. While generating the token, these are getting validated and yes, we are validating with the database directly. Let's see how.

`IdentityServer4` provides two interfaces for this purpose, named `IProfileService` and `IResourceOwnerPasswordValidator`.

The following is a `ResourceOwnerPasswordValidator` class implementing the interface. Remember, we set `AllowedGrantTypes` = `GrantTypes.ResourceOwnerPassword` inside the config for the client. That's why we are doing this to validate the user's credentials:

```
public class ResourceOwnerPasswordValidator :
IResourceOwnerPasswordValidator
{
  private readonly FlixOneStoreContext _context;
  public ResourceOwnerPasswordValidator(FlixOneStoreContext context)
  {
    _context = context;
  }
  public async Task ValidateAsync(ResourceOwnerPassword
  ValidationContext context)
  {
    try
    {
      var customer = await _context.Customers.SingleOrDefaultAsync
      (m => m.Email == context.UserName);
      if (customer != null)
      {
        if (customer.Password == context.Password)
        {
          context.Result = new GrantValidationResult(
            subject: customer.Id.ToString(),
            authenticationMethod: "database",
            claims: GetUserClaims(customer));
          return;
        }
        context.Result = new GrantValidationResult
        (TokenRequestErrors.InvalidGrant,
        "Incorrect password");
        return;
      }
      context.Result = new GrantValidationResult
      (TokenRequestErrors.InvalidGrant,
      "User does not exist.");
      return;
```

```
      }
      catch (Exception ex)
      {
        context.Result = new GrantValidationResult
        (TokenRequestErrors.InvalidGrant,
        "Invalid username or password");
      }
    }
    public static Claim[] GetUserClaims(Customers customer)
    {
      return new Claim[]
      {
        new Claim(JwtClaimTypes.Id, customer.Id.ToString() ?? ""),
        new Claim(JwtClaimTypes.Name, (
        !string.IsNullOrEmpty(customer.Firstname) &&
        !string.IsNullOrEmpty(customer.Lastname))
        ? (customer.Firstname + " " + customer.Lastname)
        : String.Empty),
        new Claim(JwtClaimTypes.GivenName, customer.Firstname ??
        string.Empty),
        new Claim(JwtClaimTypes.FamilyName, customer.Lastname ??
        string.Empty),
        new Claim(JwtClaimTypes.Email, customer.Email ?? string.Empty)
      };
    }
  }
```

Mark the bold lines on the preceding code. `ValidateAsync` is the method that is giving us the details from the request, and then it is verified with the database value. If matched, we create a `GrantValidationResult` object with `subject`, `authenticationMethod`, and `claims`.

`GetUserClaims` helps us build all the claims. We will see the actual use of these claims in a moment.

 We added a number of claims inside config with a list of `ApiResources`, such as `Id`, `Name`, `Email`, `GivenName`, and `FamilyName`. That means the server can return these details about the *customer*.

Let's jump to `ProfileService`:

```
public class ProfileService : IProfileService
{
  private readonly FlixOneStoreContext _context;
  public ProfileService(FlixOneStoreContext context)
```

```
    {
      _context = context;
    }
    public async Task GetProfileDataAsync(ProfileDataRequestContext
    profileContext)
    {
      if (!string.IsNullOrEmpty(profileContext.Subject.Identity.Name))
      {
        var customer = await _context.Customers
        .SingleOrDefaultAsync(m => m.Email ==
        profileContext.Subject.Identity.Name);
        if (customer != null)
        {
          var claims = ResourceOwnerPasswordValidator.
          GetUserClaims(customer);
          profileContext.IssuedClaims = claims.Where(x =>
          profileContext.RequestedClaimTypes.Contains(x.Type)).ToList();
        }
      }
      else
      {
        var customerId = profileContext.Subject.Claims.FirstOrDefault
        (x => x.Type == "sub");
        if (!string.IsNullOrEmpty(customerId.Value))
        {
          var customer = await _context.Customers
          .SingleOrDefaultAsync(u => u.Id ==
          Guid.Parse(customerId.Value));
          if (customer != null)
          {
            var claims =
            ResourceOwnerPasswordValidator.GetUserClaims(customer);
            profileContext.IssuedClaims = claims.Where(x =>
            profileContext.RequestedClaimTypes.Contains(x.Type).
            ToList();
          }
        }
      }
    }
  }
```

A `ProfileDataRequestContext` object is populated with all the claims we added in
`ApiResource`. Refer to the following screenshot of the list of claims requested while
debugging:

```
0 references | 0 exceptions
public async Task GetProfileDataAsync(ProfileDataRequestContext profileContext)
{
    try                                              profileContext [IdentityServer4.Models.ProfileDataRequestContext]
    {   ≤ 2,410ms elapsed                        Caller         "ClaimsProviderAccessToken"
                                                  Client         "htmlClient"
        if (!string.IsNullOrEmpty(profileContext.Subject.     IssuedClaims    Count = 0
        {                                         RequestedClaimTypes  {System.Linq.Enumerable.DistinctIterator<string>}
                                                  Current         null
            var customer = await _context.Customers  Non-Public members
                .SingleOrDefaultAsync(m => m.Email == prof  Results View    Expanding the Results View will enumerate the IEnumerable
                                                [0]  "id"
        if (customer != null)                     [1]  "email"
                                                  [2]  "name"
                                                  [3]  "given_name"
                                                  [4]  "family_name"
```

That means we need to fill all these details from the *customer* record that we did and add that to `IssuedClaims`.

Hold on a second! Why are we doing this? Because our config told us to provide this information. But do we need to fill in all that requested information? No. Not necessarily. We can issue as many, or as few, claims as we wish to.

The big question now! Where do we find this information? We know that after all these authorization setups, we get an encrypted token string. Did you guess? Yes, all that information actually resides inside the token itself. Don't trust me, trust the following screenshot. As the token is a JWT token, you can use https://jwt.io/ to decode it and see what is inside:

```json
{
  "nbf": 1525716685,
  "exp": 1525720285,
  "iss": "http://localhost:57571",
  "aud": [
    "http://localhost:57571/resources",
    "FlixOneStore.ReadAccess"
  ],
  "client_id": "htmlClient",
  "sub": "910d4c2f-b394-4578-8d9c-7ca3fd3266e2",
  "auth_time": 1525716684,
  "idp": "local",
  "id": "910d4c2f-b394-4578-8d9c-7ca3fd3266e2",
  "name": "Tadit Dash",
  "given_name": "Tadit",
  "family_name": "Dash",
  "email": "taditdash@gmail.com",
  "scope": [
    "FlixOneStore.ReadAccess"
  ],
  "amr": [
    "database"
  ]
}
```

Client-based API-consumption architecture

We have discussed *RESTful Services, Web APIs,* as well as how to register, authenticate, and authorize a user. Moreover, we did focus a little on the consumption aspect of the service. Services are designed not only to test on *Postman* but actually for consumption by different types of application (desktop, web, mobile, smart watches, and IoT apps).

While most modern apps are based on MVC-based architecture, there is a certain need to consume web services inside the controllers of those apps. Basically, I need to find a way to call the services from my controller without any hassle.

For that to happen, I can't call *Postman* or any other third-party tool. What I need is a client or component that can interact with the *RESTful Web API* for me. I just need to tell that client that I need the *Customer* details by passing the `id` or some identifier and the rest is taken care of by the client, from calling the API, passing the value to it, and getting the response. The response eventually comes back to the controller, which I can then operate on.

We will explore how to build a REST client with simple, quick, and easy steps in `Chapter 10`, *Building a Web Client (Consuming Web Services)*.

Summary

Registration is a very common, yet very important part of an application. We handled the registration of *Customers* through the API. Before that, we learned to bootstrap the API controller actions and model classes with EF Core. While we were doing all this, we landed on CORS and learned how to handle that, too.

Gradually, we moved to the authentication part, where we discussed *Basic Authentication* in detail. It is a mechanism to validate the client by the *Customer* (who are users of our API) credentials (`username` and `password`), which are passed in with the requests.

Bearer or *Token-based* Authentication was the next topic we explored, and we implemented the OAuth paradigm using *IdentityServer4*. In this case, the client can't access a resource directly by `username` and `password` as it was in the case of basic. What it needs is a token first, which is generated by one Authorization Server upon request by the client with client details such as *client id* and *client secret*. The token, then, can be sent to the API for subsequent requests for restricted resource access.

In the next chapter, we will take all this knowledge to build other components of our API, such as *Cart*, *Shipment*, *Order Items*, and *Checkout*.

4

Item Catalogue, Cart, and Checkout

This chapter will take a look at coding the main sections of an e-commerce app and its related API endpoints.

We have already discussed user registration and authentication in the previous chapter, and we will be carrying forward that knowledge to help us implement security inside different controllers that we build in this chapter.

To display products and search for them efficiently, we are also going to design `ProductsController`.

After that, we will also look at how to put your products into your shopping cart, discussing how to add, update, and delete items in a cart.

Last, but not least, we will also take a look at order management and processing.

In this chapter, we will cover the following topics:

- Implementing different controllers
- Product listing and product searching
- Adding, updating, and deleting cart items
- Imposing security on controllers
- Order processing and shipping information

Implementing controllers

As we are going to learn about the core functions of our app, we need to design its controllers so that we have REST endpoints to perform tasks from our client. Things such as *product listing*, *product searching*, *add to cart*, *placing orders*, and *processing shipments* can be done with one dedicated controller for each function. These controllers will be responsible for performing actions on the database, so we need to model classes for the related tables. Let's get to work!

Generating models

The following line can be executed inside the Package Manager Console to generate model classes for all the tables in the database:

```
Scaffold-DbContext
"Server=.;Database=FlixOneStore;Trusted_Connection=True;"
Microsoft.EntityFrameworkCore.SqlServer -OutputDir Models -Force
```

The preceding command will populate class files for each table inside the `Models` folder, as shown in the following screenshot:

If you have not already done so, please refer to the database script in `https://github.com/PacktPublishing/Building-RESTful-Web-services-with-DOTNET-Core` to generate the database table for your application.

Generating controllers

To generate controllers for the models, right-click on `Controllers` folder | **Add** | **Controller** | **API Controller with actions, using Entity Framework**.

First, let's start with `ProductsdetailsController`, as we want to show the products list to our customers initially.

The `Productsdetail.cs` model class generated through scaffolding should look like the following snippet:

```
public partial class Productsdetail
{
    public Guid Id { get; set; }
    public Guid? Productid { get; set; }
    public string Name { get; set; }
    public string Description { get; set; }
    public string Url { get; set; }
    public int Views { get; set; }
    public Products Product { get; set; }
}
```

The preceding code can also be used to generate the controller with GET, POST, PUT, and DELETE action methods: (We're focusing on the `GetProductsdetail` method for now.)

```
// GET: api/Productsdetails
[HttpGet]
public IEnumerable<Productsdetail> GetProductsdetail()
{
    return _context.Productsdetail;
}
```

You can quickly test whether your controller is working using Postman, as shown in the following screenshot:

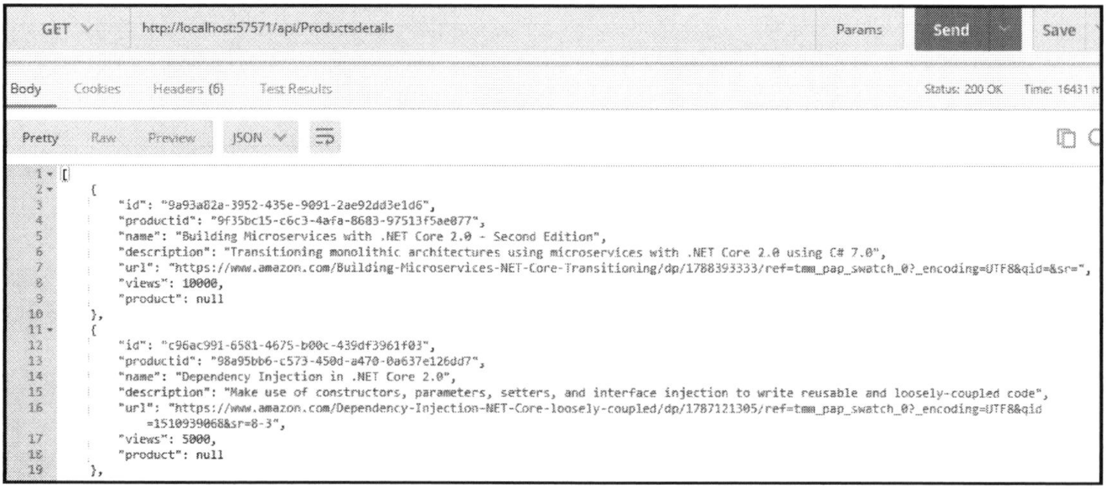

Here, the URL is `http://localhost:57571/api/Productsdetails` and the type is `GET`. We can see the results in the result box, which shows us an array of product details in a JSON format. Note that we sent this request by setting the `contentType` header with the value `application/json` inside the request's **Header** tab.

Product listing

Let's now design the jQuery code needed to consume this endpoint so that we can show these records on a web page and list our products available to buy. This should look as follows:

```
function LoadProducts()
{
  // Load products' details.
  $.ajax({
    url: 'http://localhost:57571/api/Productsdetails',
    type: "GET",
    contentType: "application/json",
    dataType: "json",
    success: function (result) {
      $.each(result, function (index, value) {
        $('#tblProducts')
          .append('<tr><td>' +
```

```
'<h3>' + value.name + '</h3>' +
'<p>' + value.description + '</p>' +
'<a target="_blank" href=' + value.url + '>Amazon Link</a>' +
'<input type="button" style="float:right;"
class="btn btn-success" value="Add To Cart" />' +
'</td></tr>');
    });
  }
});
}
```

To get the code to call the API in different languages, you can click on the *code* link inside Postman and then select the desired language. We have already discussed this in previous chapters.

The preceding method makes a call to the endpoint `http://localhost:57571/api/Productsdetails` and loops through the records after receiving them with the `success` method. While looping, it builds an HTML table row that appends to a pre-existing table on the page.

The following screenshot is the reflection of the jQuery code which is showing the details of all products:

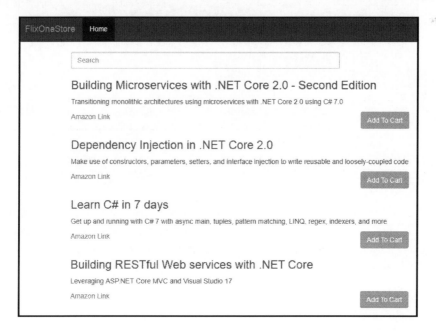

Notice that we have one **Search** box at the top, as well as **Add To Cart** buttons for each product. We will take a look at these functionalities later on.

Did you notice that the product's main parameter, the price, is not displayed? This is because the price isn't present in the Productdetail table. So, let's now take a look at the Product.cs model class, as follows:

```
public partial class Products
{
  public Products()
  {
    Cart = new HashSet<Cart>();
    CartAttributes = new HashSet<CartAttributes>();
    OrdersProducts = new HashSet<OrdersProducts>();
    ProductsAttributes = new HashSet<ProductsAttributes>();
    Productsdetail = new HashSet<Productsdetail>();
    Reviews = new HashSet<Reviews>();
  }
  public Guid Id { get; set; }
  public int Qty { get; set; }
  public string Model { get; set; }
  public string Image { get; set; }
  public decimal Price { get; set; }
  public DateTime Addedon { get; set; }
  public DateTime Modifiedon { get; set; }
  public decimal Weight { get; set; }
  public byte Status { get; set; }
  public Guid? ManufactureId { get; set; }
  public Guid? Taxclassid { get; set; }
  public ICollection<Cart> Cart { get; set; }
  public ICollection<CartAttributes> CartAttributes { get; set; }
  public ICollection<OrdersProducts> OrdersProducts { get; set; }
  public ICollection<ProductsAttributes> ProductsAttributes
  { get; set; }
  public ICollection<Productsdetail> Productsdetail { get; set; }
  public ICollection<Reviews> Reviews { get; set; }
}
```

Clearly, the Product class contains everything we need including Name, Description, Url, Views, and so on, with Productdetail as a reference point. We have already consumed the GET action of ProductdetailsController to display our products, so now it's time to read all of our products using ProductsController.

The GET action of ProductsController would return us all of the product records in Productdetail, as follows:

```
// GET: api/Products
[HttpGet]
public IEnumerable<Products> GetProducts()
{
    return _context.Products.Include(x => x.Productsdetail).ToList();
}
```

The snippet in bold in the preceding code is the Include clause, which is used to include results from the Productdetail. Now, instead of calling /api/Productsdetails, we will call /api/Products.

Calling this endpoint won't actually work, this is because of circular reference. If you observe both the Products and Productdetail models closely, you should see that both contain references to each other. This creates a problem when parsing to JSON. To avoid this, we need to write the following code inside Startup:

services.AddMvc()
.AddJsonOptions(options =>
{
options.SerializerSettings.ReferenceLoopHandling =
ReferenceLoopHandling.Ignore;
});

Let's now have a look at the response we receive for one product when we call this endpoint, as shown in the following snippet. Note that you would get an array in reality, but we are only showing you one record for brevity:

```
{
    "id": "98a95bb6-c573-450d-a470-0a637e126dd7",
    "qty": 30,
    "model": "A",
    "image": "NA",
    "price": 49.99,
    "addedon": "2018-05-13T12:09:39.873",
    "modifiedon": "2018-05-13T12:09:39.873",
    "weight": 0.9,
    "status": 1,
    "manufactureId": null,
    "taxclassid": null,
    "cart": [],
    "cartAttributes": [],
    "ordersProducts": [],
```

```
"productsAttributes": [],
"productsdetail": [
{
  "id": "c96ac991-6581-4675-b00c-439df3961f03",
  "productid": "98a95bb6-c573-450d-a470-0a637e126dd7",
  "name": "Dependency Injection in .NET Core 2.0",
  "description": "Make use of constructors, parameters,
  setters, and interface injection to write reusable and
  loosely-coupled code",
  "url": "https://www.amazon.com/Dependency-Injection-NET-Core-
  loosely-coupled/dp/1787121305/ref=tmm_pap_swatch_0?
  _encoding=UTF8&qid=1510939068&sr=8-3",
  "views": 5000
}],
"reviews": []
}
```

Now, we need to alter our client-side code to reflect the fact that Productdetail is now inside the Product object, as follows:

```
function LoadProducts()
{
  // Load products' details.
  $.ajax({
    url: 'http://localhost:57571/api/Products',
    type: "GET",
    contentType: "application/json",
    dataType: "json",
    success: function (result) {
      console.log(result);
      $.each(result, function (index, value) {
        $('#tblProducts')
        .append('<tr><td>' +
        '<h3>' + value.productsdetail[0].name + '</h3>' +
        '<span class="spanPrice">Price: $' + value.price +
        '</span>' +
        '<p>' + value.productsdetail[0].description + '</p>' +
        '<a target="_blank" href=' + value.productsdetail[0].url +
        '>Amazon Link</a>' +
        '<input type="button" style="float:right;" class="btn btn-
        success" value="Add To Cart" />' +
        '</td></tr>');
      });
    }
  });
}
```

That was easy to understand, wasn't it? Here, you should notice the changes we made to the URL and how we read the product details. `Productsdetail` is inside the `Product` object as an array, so it is written as `value.productsdetail[0]`, where `value` is the product object. We also introduced `value.price`.

You should now see the following screenshot, which has been updated:

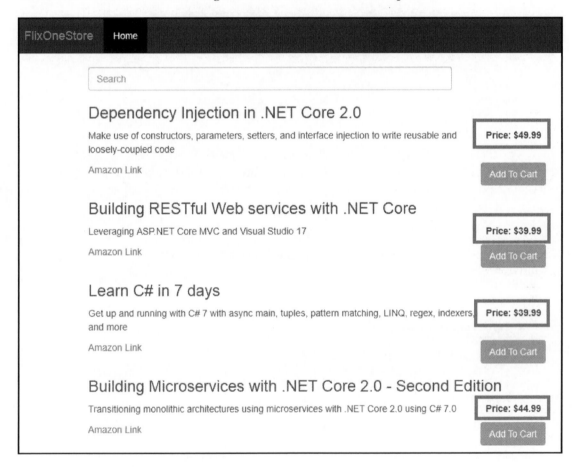

Product searching

It's now time to implement the search feature, allowing customers to put any string inside the search box to look up a product. We need to add one search button to the UI, which when clicked will receive the entered string and fetch records accordingly.

Firstly, the `action` method needs to accept the search text entered by a customer as a parameter; currently, `GetProducts()` does not accept any parameter.

The updated `GetProducts()` should look like the following snippet:

```
// GET: api/Products
[HttpGet]
public IEnumerable<Products> GetProducts(string searchText)
{
  var products = _context.Products.Include(x =>
  x.Productsdetail).ToList();
  if (!string.IsNullOrEmpty(searchText))
  products = products.Where(p => p.Productsdetail
  .Any(pd => pd.Name.ToLower().Contains(searchText.ToLower())))
  .ToList();
  return products;
}
```

The `searchText` parameter is taken into consideration and the results are filtered by the title of a book, which resides in the `Name` field of the `Productsdetail` collection inside the `Product` object. Thus, `Any` is used to check if the `searchText` is present in the `Productsdetail` object.

Now that the API is ready to search, let's update the client-side code to send the parameter as follows:

```
function LoadProducts(searchText)
{
  if (!searchText)
  searchText = "";
  // Load products' details.
  $.ajax({
    url: 'http://localhost:57571/api/Products?searchText=' +
    searchText,
    type: "GET",
    // Other codes removed for brevity.
```

As you can see in the preceding snippet, `LoadProducts` now accepts a `searchText` parameter that is passed to the API as a URL parameter. Now it is just a matter of sending the parameter value to this method while calling.

The following code illustrates the search function as it fetches text and executes LoadProducts with the entered value:

```
$('#btnSearch').click(function ()
{
  var searchText = $('#txtSearch').val().trim();
  if (searchText)
  {
    $('#tblProducts').empty();
    LoadProducts(searchText);
  }
});
```

The following screenshot shows this function in action:

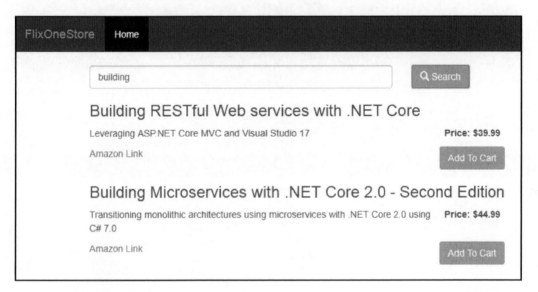

Adding to cart

We're now ready for the next important topic: all about adding to cart! Before implementing this function, however, there is something worth taking note of. In our application, we are not going to allow unknown users to add to cart, as we will be storing any information related to the cart in our database.

Implementing security

This is where security comes in, namely, authentication. As discussed in Chapter 3, *User Registration and Administration*, basic authentication can be applied with the help of handlers, or bearer authentication can be applied with the help of tokens.

First, let's generate CartsController using the same steps as previously. We now need to apply the [Authorize] attribute to the controller directly, so that all operations in the cart can be authenticated. Our app is already set up to handle bearer authentication.

The following is a code snapshot of CartsController:

```
[Produces("application/json")]
[Route("api/Carts")]
[Authorize]
public class CartsController : Controller
```

Due to the [Authorize] attribute, this controller won't allow you to access the GET, POST, PUT, and DELETE action methods if you don't provide the access token.

Let's start designing some cart-related functions on the client side and try to call the action methods in this controller, as shown in the following screenshot:

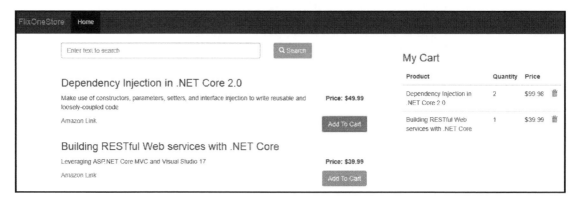

Client-side AddToCart function

When a customer hits **Add To Cart**, information is added to another HTML table called **My Cart**. If you hit **Add To Cart** twice for one product, its quantity is updated to **2** and the price is calculated accordingly. Each click assumes one unit of a particular product.

Let's now dive into the code. The following snippet shows us the AddToCart function for JavaScript:

```
function AddToCart(productId, productName, qty, price)
{
  $('#tblCart tbody')
  .append($('<tr>')
    .attr('data-product-id', productId)
    .append($('<td>').html(productName))
    .append($('<td class="qty">').html(qty))
    .append($('<td class="price">').html('$' + qty * price))
    .append($('<td>')
      .append($('<a>')
        .attr('href', '#')
        .append($('<span>').addClass('glyphicon glyphicon-trash'))
        // For Delete Icon.
        .click(function ()
        {
          // Delete Cart from Database.
        })
      )
    )
  );
  // Add one Cart record in Database.
}
```

This function takes the parameters productId, productName, qty, and price as this information is shown in the cart HTML table.

Notice, in the preceding image, that there is a delete icon in each row. This is produced by adding a glyphicon inside a span that is wrapped with an anchor whose click event is also defined. We will take a look at the delete functionality later on in this chapter.

Also, note the data-product-id attribute that has been added to the row. This helps us identify a cart row uniquely, and you will see how that helps in a moment.

We are now all set to call `CartsController` to insert cart details into the database. However, we still need one more thing inside this method. After all, what happens if a product is added to the cart unexpectedly?

Here, we need the opportunity to update the cart, instead of just adding products to it, as shown in the following snippet:

```
function AddToCart(productId, productName, qty, price)
{
  // Check if item already present. If yes, increase the qty
  and calculate price.
  var cartItem = $('#tblCart').find('tr[data-product-id=' +
  productId + ']');
  if (cartItem.length > 0)
  {
    var qtyTd = cartItem.find('td.qty');
    var newQty = parseInt(qtyTd.html()) + qty;
    qtyTd.html(newQty);
    cartItem.find('td.price').html('$' + (newQty * price).toFixed(2));
    // Update Cart in Database: PUT /api/Carts/{id}
    return;
  }
  $('#tblCart tbody')
  .append($('<tr>')
    .attr('data-product-id', productId)
    .append($('<td>').html(productName))
    .append($('<td class="qty">').html(qty))
    .append($('<td class="price">').html('$' + qty * price))
    .append($('<td>')
      .append($('<a>')
        .attr('href', '#')
        .append($('<span>').addClass('glyphicon glyphicon-trash'))
        .click(function () {
          // Delete Cart from Database: DELETE /api/Carts/{id}
        })
      )
    )
  );
  // Add one Cart record in Database: POST /api/Carts
}
```

Simple, isn't it? First, the record is fetched from the cart table with the help of a product ID and then its quantity and price is updated accordingly. From that block, a `return` statement ensures that the record isn't added to the table anymore.

Now everything should work on the client side. We now just need to call our APIs to involve database operations so that any rows that have been inserted, updated, and deleted are also updated on the server side.

API calls for AddToCart

In this section, we will take a look at the actual API calls made by the client.

POST – api/Carts

Inserting data into the cart table can be done by calling the POST action, which should look like the following code block in CartsController:

```
// POST: api/Carts
[HttpPost]
public async Task<IActionResult> PostCart([FromBody] Cart cart)
{
  if (!ModelState.IsValid)
  {
    return BadRequest(ModelState);
  }
  _context.Cart.Add(cart);
  try
  {
    await _context.SaveChangesAsync();
  }
  catch (DbUpdateException)
  {
    if (CartExists(cart.Id))
    {
      return new StatusCodeResult(StatusCodes.Status409Conflict);
    }
    else
    {
      throw;
    }
  }
  return CreatedAtAction("GetCart", new { id = cart.Id }, cart);
}
```

The client-side function to call this action can be designed as follows:

```
function PostCart(customerId, productId, qty, finalPrice)
{
  var cart =
  {
    Customerid: customerId,
    Productid: productId,
    Qty: qty,
    Finalprice: finalPrice
  };
  $.ajax({
    url: 'http://localhost:57571/api/Carts',
    type: "POST",
    contentType: "application/json",
    dataType: "json",
    data: JSON.stringify(cart),
    success: function (result) {
      console.log(result);
    },
    error: function (message) {
      console.log(message.statusText);
    }
  });
}
```

Straightforward, isn't it? Now we can build a cart object and send it a POST action. You can try this out by calling the following method inside our AddToCart() function:

```
// Add one Cart record in Database: POST /api/Carts
PostCart('910D4C2F-B394-4578-8D9C-7CA3FD3266E2',
  productId,
  cartItem.find('td.qty').html(),
  cartItem.find('td.price').html().replace('$', ''))
```

Here, the first parameter is Customerid, which we have hard-coded. Customerid can be held in session storage for any requests—although this is considered a risky practice.

Instead of sending the Customerid, you can send the email id to the POST action. Then using email id, you can get the Customerid, which can be used to insert a Cart record.

Let's now run our app and click on **Add To Cart** for a particular product. Oops! The following error has appeared in the developer tool:

```
function PostCart(customerId, productId, qty, finalPrice) {
    var cart = {
        Customerid: customerId,
        Productid: productId,
        Qty: qty,
        Finalprice: finalPrice
    };

    $.ajax({
        url: 'http://localhost:57571/api/Carts',
        type: "POST",
        contentType: "application/json",
        dataType: "json",
        data: JSON.stringify(cart),
        success: function (result) {
            console.log(result);
        },
        error: function (message) { message = {readyState: 4,
            console.log(message.statusText);            "Unauthorized"
        }
    });
```

Why has this happened?

The reason for this error is actually pretty obvious. As an [Authorize] attribute has been applied to the controller, every call to CartsController now expects a token generated by a request to the OAuth2.0 Authorize server with Email Id and Password.

> We already explored *OAuth2.0 Authentication* in detail.

To move on with our implementation, we will call the token server from Postman and use that inside our app. Ideally, when you receive an **Unauthorized** error, you should open the login screen so that the user can log in. If Email Id and Password are validated, a token would be returned. This token can be used for further requests, such as **Add To Cart**.

To save time and space, we will generate a token using Postman directly by using `taditdash@gmail.com` as our email ID and `12345` as our password. The subsequent Ajax call with the token should look like the following:

```
$.ajax({
  url: 'http://localhost:57571/api/Carts',
  type: "POST",
  contentType: "application/json",
  dataType: "json",
  data: JSON.stringify(cart),
  headers: { "Authorization": "Bearer eyJhbGciOiJSUzI1NiIs...
  [Long String Removed]" },
  success: function (result)
  {
    var cartItem = $('#tblCart').find('tr[data-product-id=' +
    productId + ']');
    cartItem.attr('data-cart-id', result.id);
  },
});
```

Note that we have removed the token string in the preceding snippet for brevity. With the previous code, one cart record will be created and data returned from the API will give us all the detail about that record. You can store the cart's `Id` on the HTML row (as shown inside the preceding code block) for further processing while updating or deleting the cart record.

The following screenshot of the **Elements** tab in the Chrome Developer Tool illustrates the cart record's ID stored as a `data-cart-id` attribute:

```
▼<table id="tblCart" class="table">
  ▶<thead>…</thead>
  ▼<tbody>
    ▼<tr data-product-id="98a95bb6-c573-450d-a470-0a637e126dd7" data-cart-id=
    "a8b64589-7e2e-4eab-8940-6865d9d32bda"> == $0
      <td>Dependency Injection in .NET Core 2.0</td>
      <td class="qty">1</td>
      <td class="price">$49.99</td>
    ▶<td>…</td>
    </tr>
  </tbody>
</table>
```

PUT – api/Carts/{id}

Now that we have added one cart record, let's move to update that record whenever a
customer repeatedly hits the **Add To Cart** button. We already have the code that updates
the quantity and price on the client-side table, so we just need to write the code to call the
PUT endpoint to update the record, as follows:

```
function PutCart(cartItem)
{
  var cart =
  {
    Id: cartItem.attr('data-cart-id'),
    Customerid: '910D4C2F-B394-4578-8D9C-7CA3FD3266E2',
    Productid: cartItem.attr('data-product-id'),
    Qty: cartItem.find('td.qty').html(),
    Finalprice: cartItem.find('td.price').html().replace('$', '')
  };
  $.ajax({
    url: 'http://localhost:57571/api/Carts/' + cart.Id,
    type: "PUT",
    contentType: "application/json",
    dataType: "json",
    data: JSON.stringify(cart),
    headers: { "Authorization": "Bearer eyJhbGciOiJSUzI1NiIs..." }
  });
}
```

The important part of the preceding code is the URL, which also contains the cart Id
because the route is actually api/Carts/{id}. The data goes inside the body.

The parameter cartItem is the row which can be passed from the AddToCart function as
follows:

```
// Update Cart in Database: PUT /api/Carts/{id}
PutCart($('#tblCart').find('tr[data-product-id=' + productId + ']'));
```

The API action should look as follows:

```
// PUT: api/Carts/5
[HttpPut("{id}")]
public async Task<IActionResult> PutCart([FromRoute] Guid id, [FromBody]
Cart cart)
{
  if (!ModelState.IsValid)
  {
    return BadRequest(ModelState);
  }
```

```
if (id != cart.Id)
{
  return BadRequest();
}
_context.Entry(cart).State = EntityState.Modified;
try
{
  await _context.SaveChangesAsync();
}
catch (DbUpdateConcurrencyException)
{
  if (!CartExists(id))
  {
    return NotFound();
  }
  else
  {
    throw;
  }
}
return NoContent();
}
```

Notice that `id` is read from the route, as it is marked with the attribute `[FromRoute]`, and the cart object is read from the body of the request, as it is marked `[FromBody]`. If an ID is not sent with a route, the client would receive a **400 BadRequest** error.

The API action has now updated the record with the necessary details, as shown in the following screenshot:

As you can see, we have clicked **Add To Cart** four times. The `finalPrice` is calculated accordingly as `49.99 * 4`.

DELETE – api/Carts/{id}

Route `/api/Carts/{id}` tells us that we just need to send the cart `Id` to the API; everything else will be handled by the API so as to delete the record from the database.

The action method for deleting a record is as follows:

```
// DELETE: api/Carts/5
[HttpDelete("{id}")]
public async Task<IActionResult> DeleteCart([FromRoute] Guid id)
{
    if (!ModelState.IsValid)
    {
        return BadRequest(ModelState);
    }
    var cart = await _context.Cart.SingleOrDefaultAsync(m => m.Id == id);
    if (cart == null)
    {
        return NotFound();
    }
    _context.Cart.Remove(cart);
    await _context.SaveChangesAsync();
    return Ok(cart);
}
```

The client-side application has to be updated to allow this feature. As the delete icon is already shown on every cart row on the HTML table, we just need to send the cart's ID to the API when clicked by the user.

The following JavaScript function can be used to delete a cart record:

```
function DeleteCart(cartId)
{
    $.ajax({
        url: 'http://localhost:57571/api/Carts/' + cartId,
        type: "DELETE",
        contentType: "application/json",
        headers: { "Authorization": "Bearer " + accessToken },
        success: function (result) {
            if (result.id) {
                // Deleting the row from the html table.
                var cartItem = $('#tblCart').find('tr[data-cart-id=' +
                cartId + ']');
                cartItem.remove();
            }
        }
    });
}
```

As you can see, the `DeleteCart` function expects one parameter, `cartId`, which will be provided when the delete icon is clicked. This function calls the API with the type `DELETE`, as well as the `Id` and URL. On successful deletion, the cart row is removed from the HTML table.

The code block where `DeleteCart` is called is inside `AddToCart`, as shown in the following code snippet:

```
cartItem = $('#tblCart tbody')
.append($('<tr>')
  .attr('data-product-id', productId)
  .append($('<td>').html(productName))
  .append($('<td class="qty">').html(qty))
  .append($('<td class="price">').html('$' + qty * price))
  .append($('<td>')
    .append($('<a>')
      .attr('href', '#')
      .append($('<span>').addClass('glyphicon glyphicon-trash'))
      .click(function () {
        // Delete Cart from Database: DELETE /api/Carts/{id}
        DeleteCart($(this).parents('tr').attr('data-cart-id'));
      })
    )
  )
);
```

`DeleteCart` is called inside the click event of the anchor where the delete icon is shown. Inside the event, we get the cart `Id` from the row itself by extracting the value of the `data-cart-id` attribute.

Placing orders

Our cart is now full with the correct number of the desired products, so it's now time to place our order. For that, we need to call another controller—`OrdersController`.

The following two tables are responsible for the ordering process:

- **Orders**: This stores the shipping address details, customer details, order status, and so on
- **OrdersProducts**: This stores the products added to the cart, their price, and their quantity

The `Orders` class is generated by the scaffolding we did initially, which contains all the necessary information. Let's generate the controller with this class. Follow the same process to generate the controller as we did for `ProductsController`, `ProductsdetailsController`, and `CartsController`.

> The model and controller class can be found in the GitHub repository.

Now it's time to call the POST action of `OrdersController` to save the order on the client-side. The following code is the skeleton of the function that does that:

```
function PostOrders()
{
    // 1. Build order object to match the model class Orders.cs.
    // 2. Push cart items into order object as an array.
    // 3. Call POST /api/Orders.
}
```

Let's now explain this step-by-step.

UI design for placing an order

Before we move on any further, we need to show a modal to the user where they can enter their shipping address. The modal will be opened once the **Place Order** button is clicked, as shown in the following screenshot.

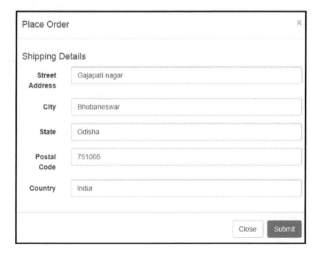

The following code snippet illustrates the click event for **Place Order** (the modal is opened if cart items are present):

```
$('#btnPlaceOrder').click(function ()
{
    var cartItems = $('#tblCart tbody tr');
    // If Cart items present, then show modal to enter Shipping Address.
    if (cartItems.length > 0) {
        $('#Order').modal('show');
        return;
    }
    alert("Please add items into the cart.");
});
```

An Ajax call inserts an order's record in the database by clicking **Submit** using POST. The following code snippet is the click event of **Submit**:

```
$('#btnConfirmOrder').click(function () {
    PostOrders();
});
```

The client-side PostOrder function

Let's now move on to the steps required for PostOrders.

Building order objects to match the model class Orders.cs

Here, we have to read the values from the text boxes related to shipping information and match them with the fields of Orders.cs to build an object. OrdersProducts is an array representing the model class, OrdersProducts.cs. Every order can have multiple products associated with it.

The following code implements order objects:

```
// 1. Build order object to match the model class Orders.cs.
var order = {
    Customerid: customerId,
    CustomerStreetaddress: $('#txtStreetAdd').val(),
    Customercity: $('#txtCity').val(),
    Customerstate: $('#txtState').val(),
    Customerpostalcode: $('#txtPostalCode').val(),
    Customercountry: $('#txtCountry').val(),
```

```
OrdersProducts: new Array()
};
```

Pushing cart items into an order object as an array

Populating the `OrdersProducts` array is the next step, and this can be done by looping through the cart table's rows and pushing each cart row's details to the array. Inside the loop, read all the necessary values from the row, either from its attribute or `td`. Remember to form an object and assign the values to field names that match the model class, as follows:

```
// 2. Push cart items into order object as an array.
$('#tblCart tbody tr').each(function ()
{
  order.OrdersProducts.push(
  {
    Productid: $(this).attr('data-product-id'),
    Productname: $(this).find('td.name').html(),
    Productprice: $(this).attr('data-price'),
    Finalprice: $(this).find('td.price').html().replace('$', ''),
    Productqty: $(this).find('td.qty').html()
  });
});
```

Calling POST /api/Orders

Great, now we have our object! It's now time to call the API `/api/Orders` with a `POST` request so that our order goes into the database, as follows:

```
// 3. Call POST /api/Orders.
$.ajax({
  url: 'http://localhost:57571/api/Orders',
  type: "POST",
  contentType: "application/json",
  dataType: "json",
  data: JSON.stringify(order),
  headers: { "Authorization": "Bearer " + accessToken },
  success: function (result) {
    alert("Order Placed Successfully.")
  }
});
```

If everything works correctly, you should see something like the following screenshot:

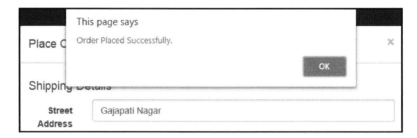

But we are forgetting something here; although our order has been placed successfully, we need to empty the cart. This can be done by calling DELETE /api/Carts for each cart item inside the success function of PostOrders, shown as follows:

```
success: function (result)
{
  // Empty Cart.
  $('#tblCart tbody tr').each(function () {
    DeleteCart($(this).attr('data-cart-id'));
  });
  alert("Order Placed Successfully.");
},
```

We've explored everything from the client side, so now it's time to check the API.

PostOrders API POST method

The **Orders** table looks a little different to what we sent to the client. In the following screenshot, note the fields marked in boxes. These are the fields we are not sending and will instead manipulate inside the action method:

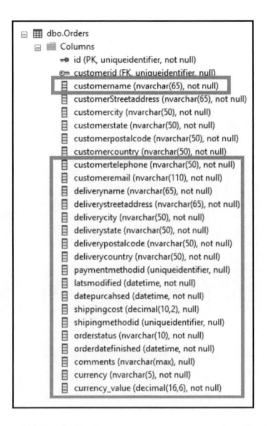

Fields such as name, email, and telephone number can be fetched from the **Customers** table. `Customerid` is sent from the client, using which we will fetch these details, as follows:

```
// POST: api/Orders
[HttpPost]
public async Task<IActionResult> PostOrders([FromBody] Orders orders)
{
  if (!ModelState.IsValid)
  {
    return BadRequest(ModelState);
  }
  // Retrieve customer details and add to order.
  if (orders.Customerid != null)
  {
    var customer = _context.Customers.SingleOrDefault
    (x => x.Id == orders.Customerid);
    if (customer != null)
    {
```

```
        orders.Deliveryname = orders.Customername = customer.Firstname;
        orders.Customeremail = customer.Email;
        orders.Customertelephone = customer.Telephone;
    }
}
...
```

The following code snippet illustrates how a user can copy their billing address so that it is also their delivery address:

```
// Copy customer address to delivery address.
orders.Deliverycity = orders.Customercity;
orders.Deliverycountry = orders.Customercountry;
orders.Deliverystreetaddress = orders.CustomerStreetaddress;
orders.Deliverypostalcode = orders.Customerpostalcode;
orders.Deliverystate = orders.Customerstate;
```

Additional fields, including `datapurchased`, `lastmodified`, and `orderdatefinished`, will be set as `DateTime.Now`. Details such as `currency` and `currency_value` will be set as dollars ($) and zero (0). We will also set `Guid.NewGuid` as `shipingmethodid` and `paymentmethodid`.

These can be made inside the Orders constructor as follows:

```
public Orders()
{
    Id = Guid.NewGuid();
    OrderProductAttributes = new HashSet<OrderProductAttributes>();
    OrdersProducts = new HashSet<OrdersProducts>();
    Datepurchased = DateTime.Now;
    Lastmodified = DateTime.Now;
    Shipingmethodid = Guid.NewGuid();
    Paymentmethodid = Guid.NewGuid();
    Shippingcost = 0;
    Orderdatefinished = DateTime.Now;
    Currency = "$";
    CurrencyValue = 0;
    Orderstatus = "Placed";
}
```

Notice that the `Orderstatus` is **Placed**. This is something that can be updated by the site when an order is ready for shipping. Subsequent statuses might include **Approved, Ready, Shipped, Delivered**, and so on. If you design the admin screen, make sure you handle this field update along with `latsmodified` and `orderdatefinished`.

The application demonstrated in this book is not production-ready. Generally, there should be a login page that works with *OAuth2.0 Authentication*. Basic validations on the API side, as well as the client side, also need to be handled. In this book, our application is built to showcase the concepts we are exploring, but you can definitely optimize our example and even build on top of it.

Exposing shipping details

GET requests can be used on OrdersController with an order ID so that order details can be consumed by third party sites for display. For example, many courier companies expose their APIs, which is used by other sites to display order, shipment, and tracking information.

As an example, let's check out our GET method OrdersController, which takes the ID as a parameter:

```
// GET: api/Orders/5
[HttpGet("{id}")]
public async Task<IActionResult> GetOrders([FromRoute] Guid id)
{
  if (!ModelState.IsValid)
  {
    return BadRequest(ModelState);
  }
  var orders = await _context.Orders.Include
  (o => o.OrdersProducts).SingleOrDefaultAsync(m => m.Id == id);
  if (orders == null)
  {
    return NotFound();
  }
  return Ok(orders);
}
```

Notice that the `Include` clause is used to include results from the `OrdersProducts` table. Let's now perform a quick Postman call to this endpoint to see the result of our earlier order, as shown in the following screenshot:

Here, you can see every detail relating to the order, along with its products, are returned from the API.

Summary

If you've reached this point of the book, you will have designed some cool things using APIs. Well done!

In this chapter, we moved towards consuming `ProductsController` to display the product list on our client-side app. Product attributes along with their pricing details were shown with a simple UI that was designed using Bootstrap, jQuery, and HTML.

Slightly modified GET requests inside `ProductsController` with a `searchString` parameter helped us to retrieve search results from the API. Clients could easily implement the search function by consuming the endpoint with text.

We then looked at our shopping cart. We explored how `CartsController` actions can be consumed to add, update, and delete cart items while updating the UI. In the process, we implemented security for the controller using authentication.

Finally, we converted the items in our cart into a visualized order. This was done using `OrdersController`, which can also be used to provide shipping and tracking information to clients.

In the next chapter, we're going to take a look at different techniques for testing the RESTful Web API designed in .NET Core.

5
Integrating External Components and Handling

So far, we have been developing our FlixOneStore. In the previous chapter, we added a shopping cart and shipping facility. However, some organizations may not need such facilities, as some organizations have everything in the house. For instance, our FlixOneStore requires an external component to help us track the assignment and payment-management system.

In this chapter, we will discuss the external components with the help of code examples. We will mainly cover the following topics:

- Understanding the middleware
- Adding logging to our API in the middleware
- Intercepting HTTP requests and responses by building our own middleware
- JSON-RPC for RPC communication

Understanding the middleware

As the name suggests, middleware is a piece of software that connects two different or similar places. In the world of software engineering, middleware is a software component and is assembled in an application pipeline to handle requests and responses.

These components can also check whether a request should pass to the next components, or whether the request should be handled by a component before or after the next component is triggered/invoked. This request pipeline is built with the use of a request delegate. This request delegate interacts with each HTTP request.

Look at the following quote from the documentation of ASP.NET Core (`https://docs.microsoft.com/en-us/aspnet/core/fundamentals/middleware/`):

> *"Middleware is software that's assembled into an application pipeline to handle requests and responses."*

Look at the following diagram, showing an example of a simple middleware component:

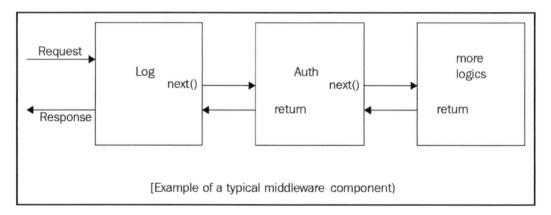

[Example of a typical middleware component)

Requesting delegates

Requests are handled by the `Use`, `Run`, `Map`, and `MapWhen` extension methods. These methods configure the request delegates.

To understand this in detail, let's create a dummy project using `ASP.NET Core`. Go through the following steps:

1. Open Visual Studio.
2. Go to **File** | **New** | **Project**, or click *Ctrl + Shift + N*. Refer to the following screenshot:

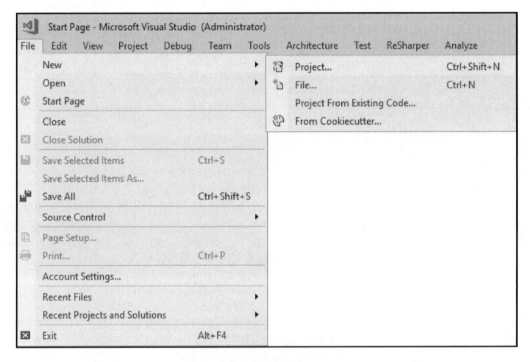

Creating a new project using Visual Studio 2017

3. From the **New Project** screen, select **ASP.NET Core Web Application**.

4. Name your new project (say `Chap05_01`), select a location, and click **OK**, as shown in the following screenshot:

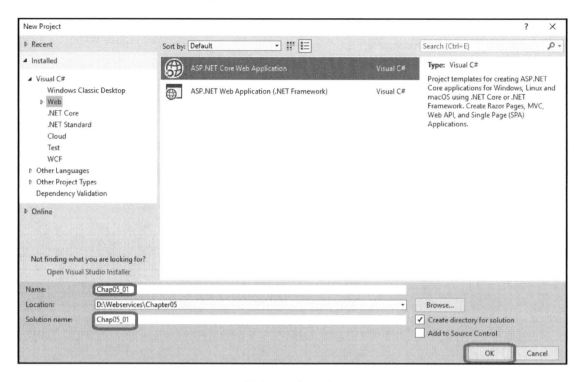

Selecting new project template

5. From the new **ASP.NET Core Web Application** template screen, choose the **API** template. Make sure you select **.NET Core** and **ASP.NET Core 2.0**.

6. Click **OK**, as shown in the following screenshot:

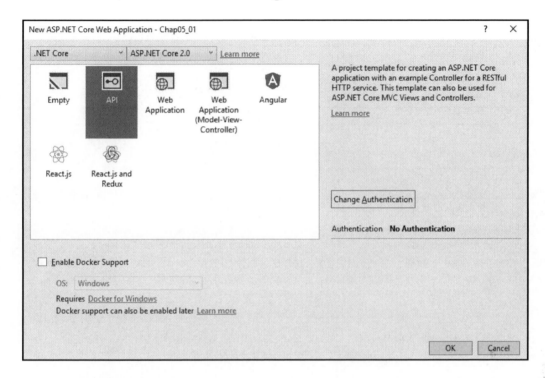

7. Open **Solution Explorer**. You will see the file/folder structure, as shown in the following screenshot:

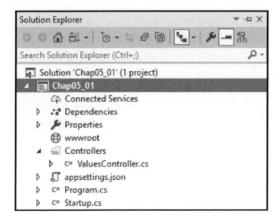

Showing file/folder structure of Chap05_01 project

From the dummy project that we have just created, open the `Startup.cs` file and look at the `Configure` method, which contains the following code:

```
// This method gets called by the runtime. Use this method to configure the
HTTP request pipeline.
public void Configure(IApplicationBuilder app, IHostingEnvironment env)
{
  if (env.IsDevelopment())
  {
    app.UseDeveloperExceptionPage();
  }
  app.UseMvc();
}
```

The preceding code is self-explanatory: it tells the system to add `Mvc` to the request pipelines by initiating the `app.UseMvc()` extension method of `Microsoft.AspNetCore.Builder.IApplicationBuilder`.

 You can get more information on `IApplicationBuilder` at `https://docs.microsoft.com/en-us/dotnet/api/microsoft.aspnetcore.builder.iapplicationbuilder?view=aspnetcore-2.0`.

It also instructs the system to use a particular exception page if the environment is in development. The preceding method configures the application.

In the next section, we will discuss four important `IApplicationBuilder` methods in detail.

Use

The `Use` method adds a delegate to the application request pipelines. Look at the following screenshot for the signature of this method:

```
(Func<RequestDelegate,RequestDelegate> middleware):IApplicationBuilder
(this IApplicationBuilder app, Func<HttpContext,Func<Task>,Task>
middleware):IApplicationBuilder
  Adds a middleware delegate defined in-line to the application's request
  pipeline.
  middleware: A function that handles the request or calls the given next
  function.
```

Signature of Use method

As we discussed in the previous section, the middleware methods can short circuit the request pipeline or pass the request to the next delegate.

 Short-circuiting a request is nothing but ending a request.

Look at the following code for the Use method:

```
public void Configure(IApplicationBuilder app)
{
    async Task Middleware(HttpContext context, Func<Task> next)
    {
        //other stuff
        await next.Invoke();
        //other stuff
    }
    app.Use(Middleware);
}
```

In the preceding code, I have tried to explain the dummy implementation of the Use method with the help of a local function. Here, you can see that Middleware is invoking or passing the request to the next delegate, before or after await next.Invoke();. You can write/implement other code phrases, but these phrases should not send responses to the client, such as those that write output, produce the 404 status, and so on.

 Local functions are the methods that are declared within a method and can be called within the scope of the method itself. These methods can only be used by another method.

Run

The Run method adds a delegate to the request pipeline in the same way as the Use method, but this method terminates the request pipeline. Look at the following screenshot for the signature of this method:

> (this IApplicationBuilder app, **RequestDelegate handler**):void
> Adds a terminal middleware delegate to the application's request pipeline.
> **handler:** A delegate that handles the request.

Look at the following code:

```
public void Configure(IApplicationBuilder app, ILoggerFactory logger)
{
   logger.AddConsole();
   //add more stuff that does not responses client
   async Task RequestDelegate(HttpContext context)
   {
      await context.Response.WriteAsync("This ends the request or
      short circuits request.");
   }
   app.Run(RequestDelegate);
}
```

In the preceding code, I tried to show that `Run` terminates the request pipeline. Here, I used a local function, `RequestDelegate`.

You can see that I added a console logger before this and that there is scope to add more code phrases, but not those phrases that send responses back to the client. Here, `Run` terminates by returning a string. Run Visual Studio or press *F5*—you will get an output similar to the following screenshot:

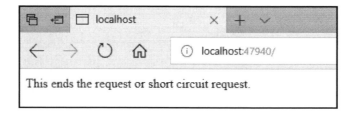

Map

The `Map` method helps when you want to connect multiple instances of middleware. To do this, `Map` calls another request delegate. Look at the following screenshot for the signature of this method:

```
Q̂₊ (extension) IApplicationBuilder IApplicationBuilder.Map(PathString pathMatch, Action<IApplicationBuilder> configuration)
Branches the request pipeline based on matches of the given request path. If the request path starts with the given path, the branch is executed.
```

Signature of Map method

Look at the following code:

```
public void Configure(IApplicationBuilder app)
{
   app.UseMvc();
   app.Map("/testroute", TestRouteHandler);
   async Task RequestDelegate(HttpContext context)
   {
      await context.Response.WriteAsync("This ends the request or
      short circuit request.");
   }
   app.Run(RequestDelegate);
}
```

In this code, I added a `Map` that just maps `<url>/testroute`. Following this is the same `Run` method that we discussed previously. `TestRoutehandler` is a private method. Look at the following code:

```
private static void  TestRouteHandler(IApplicationBuilder app)
{
   async Task Handler(HttpContext context)
   {
      await context.Response.WriteAsync("This is called from testroute.
      " + "This ends the request or short circuit request.");
   }
   app.Run(Handler);
}
```

Before `app.Run(Handler);` is a normal delegate. Now, run the code and look at the results. They should be similar to the following screenshot:

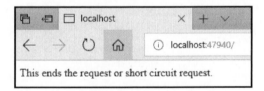

You can see that the root of the web application is showing the string that is mentioned in the `Run` delegate method. You will get the output shown in the following screenshot:

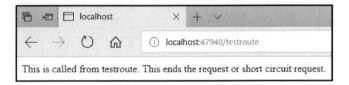

Adding logging to our API in middleware

In simple words, logging is nothing but the process or act of getting log files in one place to get the events or other actions that occur in APIs during communication. In this section, we will implement logging for our product APIs.

Before we start looking at how to log our APIs' events, let's first take a quick look at our existing product APIs.

 Refer to the *Request delegates* section to refresh your memory as to how you can create a new ASP.NET Core project.

The following screenshot shows the project structure of our product APIs:

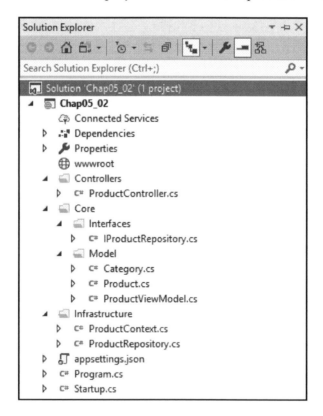

Here is our `Product` model:

```
public class Product
{
  public Guid Id { get; set; }
  public string Name { get; set; }
  public string Description { get; set; }
  public string Image { get; set; }
  public decimal Price { get; set; }
  public Guid CategoryId { get; set; }
  public virtual Category Category { get; set; }
}
```

The `Product` model is a class that represents a product, containing properties.

Here is our repository interface:

```
public interface IProductRepository
{
  void Add(Product product);
  IEnumerable<Product> GetAll();
  Product GetBy(Guid id);
  void Remove(Guid id);
  void Update(Product product);
}
```

The `IProductRepository` interface has methods that are required for our APIs to start with operations for a product.

Let's take a look at our `ProductRepository` class:

```
public class ProductRepository : IProductRepository
{
  private readonly ProductContext _context;
  public ProductRepository(ProductContext context) =>
  _context = context;
  public IEnumerable<Product> GetAll() => _context.Products.
  Include(c => c.Category).ToList();
  public Product GetBy(Guid id) => _context.Products.Include
  (c => c.Category).FirstOrDefault(x => x.Id == id);
  public void Add(Product product)
  {
    _context.Products.Add(product);
    _context.SaveChanges();
  }
  public void Update(Product product)
  {
```

```
      _context.Update(product);
      _context.SaveChanges();
    }
    public void Remove(Guid id)
    {
      var product = GetBy(id);
      _context.Remove(product);
      _context.SaveChanges();
    }
  }
}
```

The ProductRepository class implements the IProductRepository interface. The preceding code is self-explanatory.

Open the Startup.cs file and add the following code:

```
services.AddScoped<IProductRepository, ProductRepository>();
services.AddDbContext<ProductContext>(
o => o.UseSqlServer(Configuration.GetConnectionString
("ProductConnection")));
services.AddSwaggerGen(swagger =>
{
  swagger.SwaggerDoc("v1", new Info { Title = "Product APIs",
  Version = "v1" });
});
```

 For Swagger support for our Product APIs, you need to add the Swashbuckle.ASPNETCore NuGet package.

Now, open the appsettings.json file and add the following code:

```
"ConnectionStrings":
{
  "ProductConnection": "Data Source=.;Initial
  Catalog=ProductsDB;Integrated
  Security=True;MultipleActiveResultSets=True"
}
```

Let's see what our `ProductController` contains:

```
[HttpGet]
[Route("productlist")]
public IActionResult GetList()
{
    return new
    OkObjectResult(_productRepository.GetAll().
    Select(ToProductvm).ToList());
}
```

The preceding code is the GET resource of our product APIs. It calls the `GetAll()` method of our `ProductRepository`, transposes the response, and returns it. In the previous code, we have already instructed the system to resolve the `IProductRepository` interface with the `ProductRepository` class. Refer to the `Startup` class.

Here is the method that transposes the response:

```
private ProductViewModel ToProductvm(Product productModel)
{
    return new ProductViewModel
    {
        CategoryId = productModel.CategoryId,
        CategoryDescription = productModel.Category.Description,
        CategoryName = productModel.Category.Name,
        ProductDescription = productModel.Description,
        ProductId = productModel.Id,
        ProductImage = productModel.Image,
        ProductName = productModel.Name,
        ProductPrice = productModel.Price
    };
}
```

The preceding code accepts a parameter of the `Product` type and then returns an object of the `ProductViewModel` type.

The following code shows how our controller constructor is injected:

```
private readonly IProductRepository _productRepository;
public ProductController(IProductRepository productRepository)
{
    _productRepository = productRepository;
}
```

In the preceding code, we injected our `ProductRepository`, and it will be automatically initialized whenever anyone calls any resources of the product APIs.

Now, you are ready to play with the application. Run the application from the menu or click *F5*. In a web browser, you can use the suffix `/swagger` to the URL of the address.

> For the complete source code, refer to the GitHub repository link at
> `https://github.com/PacktPublishing/Building-RESTful-Web-`
> `services-with-DOTNET-Core`.

It will show the Swagger API documentation, as shown in the following screenshot:

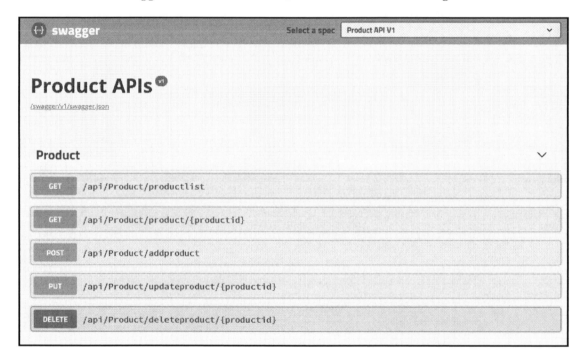

Click on the GET /api/Product/productlist resource. It will return a list of products, as shown in the following screenshot:

```
Response body
[
    {
        "productId": "02341321-c20b-48b1-a2be-47e67f548f0f",
        "productName": "Microservices for .NET",
        "productDescription": "Microservices for .NET Core",
        "productImage": "microservices.jpeg",
        "productPrice": 651,
        "categoryId": "5ccaa9d0-e436-4d1e-a463-b45696d73a9f",
        "categoryName": "Books",
        "categoryDescription": "Technical Books"
    },
    {
        "productId": "4d261e4a-a657-4add-a0f6-dde6e1464d55",
        "productName": "Learn C#",
        "productDescription": "Leanr C# in 7 days",
        "productImage": "csharp.jpeg",
        "productPrice": 520,
        "categoryId": "5ccaa9d0-e436-4d1e-a463-b45696d73a9f",
        "categoryName": "Books",
        "categoryDescription": "Technical Books"
    }
]
```

Let's implement logging for our API. Please note that to make our demo short and simple, I am not adding complex scenarios to track everything. I am adding simple logs to showcase the logging capabilities.

To start implementing logging for our product APIs, add a new class called LogAction in a new folder called Logging. Here is the code from the LogAction class:

```
public class LogActions
{
    public const int InsertProduct = 1000;
    public const int ListProducts = 1001;
    public const int GetProduct = 1002;
    public const int RemoveProduct = 1003;
}
```

The preceding code contains constants that are nothing but our application's actions, also called **events**.

Update our `ProductController`; it should now look like the following code:

```
private readonly IProductRepository _productRepository;
private readonly ILogger _logger;
public ProductController(IProductRepository productRepository, ILogger
logger)
{
  _productRepository = productRepository;
  _logger = logger;
}
```

In the preceding code, we added an `ILogger` interface, which comes from a dependency injection container (see `https://docs.microsoft.com/en-us/aspnet/core/fundamentals/dependency-injection?view=aspnetcore-2.0` for more details).

Let's add the logging capability to the `GET` resource of the product API:

```
[HttpGet]
[Route("productlist")]
public IActionResult GetList()
{
  _logger.LogInformation(LogActions.ListProducts, "Getting all
  products.");
  return new
  OkObjectResult(_productRepository.GetAll().Select(ToProductvm).
  ToList());
}
```

The preceding code returns the product list and logs the information.

To test this scenario, we need a client or an API tool so we can see the output. To do this, we will use the `Postman` extension (see `https://www.getpostman.com/` for more details).

First, we need to run the application. To do so, open the Visual Studio command prompt, move to your project folder, and then pass the command `dotnet run`. You will see a similar message to the one shown in the following screenshot:

```
D:\Webservices\Chapter05\02 Logging\Chap05_02>dotnet run
Using launch settings from D:\Webservices\Chapter05\02 Logging\Chap05_02\Properties\launchSettings.json...
Hosting environment: Development
Content root path: D:\Webservices\Chapter05\02 Logging\Chap05_02
Now listening on: http://localhost:60431
Application started. Press Ctrl+C to shut down.
```

Now, launch Postman and invoke the GET /api/product/productlist resource:

By clicking the **Send** button, you would expect a list of products to be returned, but this is not the case, as shown in the following screenshot:

> An unhandled exception occurred while processing the request.
>
> InvalidOperationException: Unable to resolve service for type 'Microsoft.Extensions.Logging.ILogger' while attempting to activate 'Chap05_02.Controllers.ProductController'.
>
> Microsoft.Extensions.Internal.ActivatorUtilities.GetService(IServiceProvider sp, Type type, Type requiredBy, bool isDefaultParameterRequired)

The preceding exception occurs because we are using a non-generic type in our ProductController that is not injectable.

So, we need to make slight changes in our ProductController. Look at the following code snippet:

```
private readonly IProductRepository _productRepository;
private readonly ILogger<ProductController> _logger;
public ProductController(IProductRepository productRepository,
ILogger<ProductController> logger)
{
  _productRepository = productRepository;
  _logger = logger;
}
```

In the preceding code, I added a generic `ILogger<ProductController>` type. As it is injectable, it will get resolved automatically.

Logging is slightly different in .NET Core 2.0 compared to its earlier versions. The implementation of the nongeneric `ILogger` is not available by default, but it is available for `ILogger<T>`. If you want to use nongeneric implementation, use `ILoggerFactory` instead of `ILogger`.

In this case, the constructor of our `ProductController` would look like the following:

```
private readonly IProductRepository _productRepository;
private readonly ILogger _logger;

public ProductController(IProductRepository
productRepository, ILoggerFactory logger)
{
_productRepository = productRepository;
_logger = logger.CreateLogger("Product logger");
}
```

Open the `Program` class and update it. It should look like the following code snippet:

```
public static void Main(string[] args)
{
  var webHost = new WebHostBuilder()
  .UseKestrel()
  .UseContentRoot(Directory.GetCurrentDirectory())
  .ConfigureAppConfiguration((hostingContext, config) =>
  {
    var env = hostingContext.HostingEnvironment;
    config.AddJsonFile("appsettings.json", optional: true,
    reloadOnChange: true)
    .AddJsonFile($"appsettings.{env.EnvironmentName}.json",
    optional: true, reloadOnChange: true);
    config.AddEnvironmentVariables();
  })
  .ConfigureLogging((hostingContext, logging) =>
  {
```

```
        logging.AddConfiguration(hostingContext.Configuration.
        GetSection("Logging"));
        logging.AddConsole();
        logging.AddDebug();
    })
    .UseStartup<Startup>()
    .Build();
    webHost.Run();
}
```

You also need to update the appsettings.json file and write more code for the logger so that your file looks like the following snippet:

```
{
    "ApplicationInsights":
    {
        "InstrumentationKey": ""
    },
    "Logging":
    {
        "IncludeScopes": false,
        "Console":
        {
            "LogLevel":
            {
                "Default": "Warning",
                "System": "Information",
                "Microsoft": "Information"
            }
        }
    },
    "ConnectionStrings":
    {
        "ProductConnection": "Data Source=.;Initial
        Catalog=ProductsDB;Integrated
        Security=True;MultipleActiveResultSets=True"
    }
}
```

Now, once again, open the Visual Studio command prompt and write the `dotnet build` command. It will build the project, and you will get a message similar to the following screenshot:

```
D:\Webservices\Chapter05\02 Logging\Chap05_02>dotnet build
Microsoft (R) Build Engine version 15.6.84.34536 for .NET Core
Copyright (C) Microsoft Corporation. All rights reserved.

  Restore completed in 87.32 ms for D:\Webservices\Chapter05\02 Logging\Chap05_02\Chap05_02.csproj.
  Restore completed in 28.26 ms for D:\Webservices\Chapter05\02 Logging\Chap05_02\Chap05_02.csproj.
  Chap05_02 -> D:\Webservices\Chapter05\02 Logging\Chap05_02\bin\Debug\netcoreapp2.0\Chap05_02.dll

Build succeeded.
    0 Warning(s)
    0 Error(s)

Time Elapsed 00:00:02.96
```

From this point, if you run Postman, it will give you the results, as shown in the following screenshot:

The preceding code adds the ability to log the actions. You will receive similar log actions to those shown in the following screenshot:

```
D:\Webservices\Chapter05\02 Logging\Chap05_02>dotnet run
Using launch settings from D:\Webservices\Chapter05\02 Logging\Chap05_02\Properties\launchSettings.json...
      info: Microsoft.AspNetCore.DataProtection.KeyManagement.XmlKeyManager[0]
      User profile is available. Using 'C:\Users\gaurav\AppData\Local\ASP.NET\DataProtection-Keys' as key reposit
ory and Windows DPAPI to encrypt keys at rest.
Hosting environment: Development
      Content root path: D:\Webservices\Chapter05\02 Logging\Chap05_02
Now listening on: http://localhost:60431
Application started. Press Ctrl+C to shut down.
info: Microsoft.AspNetCore.Hosting.Internal.WebHost[1]
      Request starting HTTP/1.1 GET http://localhost:60431/api/Product/productlist
info: Microsoft.AspNetCore.Mvc.Internal.ControllerActionInvoker[1]
      Executing action method Chap05_02.Controllers.ProductController.GetList (Chap05_02) with arguments ((null))
  - ModelState is Valid
info: Microsoft.EntityFrameworkCore.Infrastructure[10403]
      Entity Framework Core 2.0.2-rtm-10011 initialized 'ProductContext' using provider 'Microsoft.EntityFramewor
kCore.SqlServer' with options: None
info: Microsoft.EntityFrameworkCore.Database.Command[20101]
      Executed DbCommand (5ms) [Parameters=[], CommandType='Text', CommandTimeout='30']
      SELECT [c].[Id], [c].[CategoryId], [c].[Description], [c].[Image], [c].[Name], [c].[Price], [c.Category].[I
d], [c.Category].[Description], [c.Category].[Name]
      FROM [Products] AS [c]
          INNER JOIN [Categories] AS [c.Category] ON [c].[CategoryId] = [c.Category].[Id]
info: Microsoft.AspNetCore.Mvc.Internal.ObjectResultExecutor[1]
      Executing ObjectResult, writing value Microsoft.AspNetCore.Mvc.ControllerContext.
      info: Microsoft.AspNetCore.Mvc.Internal.ControllerActionInvoker[2]
      Executed action Chap05_02.Controllers.ProductController.GetList (Chap05_02) in 411.8216ms
      info: Microsoft.AspNetCore.Hosting.Internal.WebHost[2]
```

Here, we have written some code that uses the default `ILogger`. We have used default methods to invoke the logger; however, there are scenarios where we need a customized logger. In the next section, we will discuss how to write middleware for a custom logger.

Intercepting HTTP requests and responses by building our own middleware

In this section, we will create our own middleware for our existing application. In this middleware, we will log all requests and responses. Let's go through the following steps:

1. Open Visual Studio.

2. Open an existing project of the Product APIs by clicking **File** | **Open** | **Project/Solution** (or pressing *Ctrl + Shift + O*), as shown in the following screenshot:

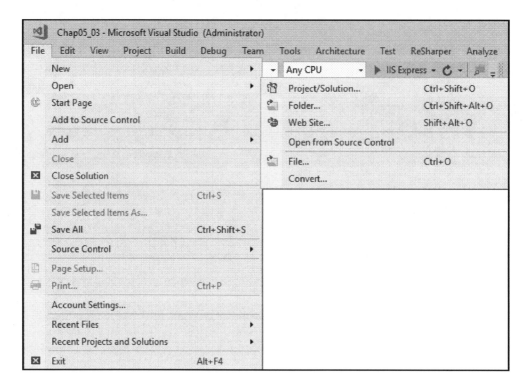

3. Locate your solution folder and click **Open**, as shown in the following screenshot:

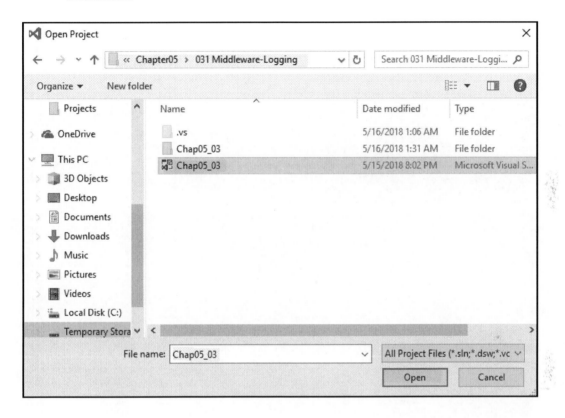

4. Open the solution explorer, add a new folder, and name it `Middleware` by right-clicking on the project name, as shown in the following screenshot:

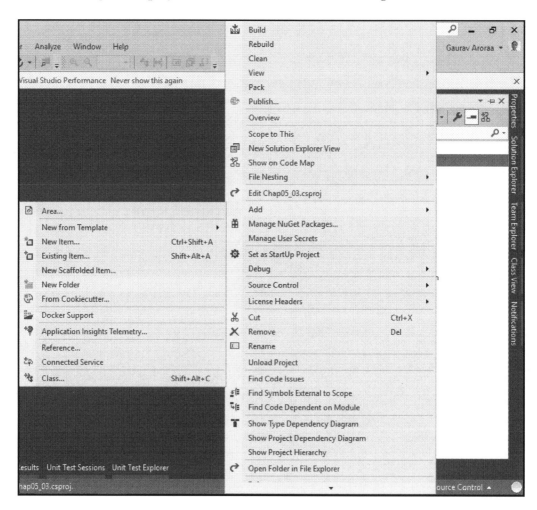

5. Right-click on the `Middleware` folder and select **Add | New Item**.
6. From the web templates, select the **Middleware Class** and name the new file `FlixOneStoreLoggerMiddleware`. Then, click **Add**, as shown in the following screenshot:

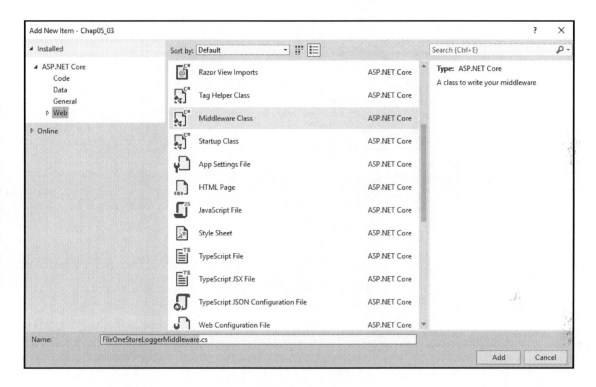

Your folder hierarchy should be like the one shown in the following screenshot:

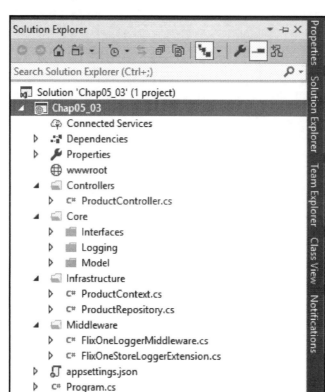

 Thanks to Justin Williams who provided a solution for POST resources; his solution is available at `https://github.com/JustinJohnWilliams/ RequestLogging`.

Look at the following code snippet of our `FlixOneStoreLoggerMiddleware` class:

```
private readonly RequestDelegate _next;
private readonly ILogger<FlixOneLoggerMiddleware> _logger;
public FlixOneLoggerMiddleware(RequestDelegate next,
ILogger<FlixOneLoggerMiddleware> logger)
{
  _next = next;
  _logger = logger;
}
```

In the preceding code, we are simply taking advantage of the inbuilt DI using the `RequestDelegate` to create our custom middleware.

The following code shows us how we should be wiring up all requests and responses for the log:

```
public async Task Invoke(HttpContext httpContext)
{
  _logger.LogInformation(await
  GetFormatedRequest(httpContext.Request));
  var originalBodyStream = httpContext.Response.Body;
  using (var responseBody = new MemoryStream())
  {
    httpContext.Response.Body = responseBody;
    await _next(httpContext);
    _logger.LogInformation(await
    GetFormatedResponse(httpContext.Response));
    await responseBody.CopyToAsync(originalBodyStream);
  }
}
```

Refer to the *Request delegate* section in this chapter, where we looked at middleware. In the preceding code, we are simply logging the request and response with the help of the `ILogger` generic type. The `await _next(httpContext);` line continues with the request pipeline.

Open the `Setup.cs` file and add the following code in the `Configure` method:

```
loggerFactory.AddConsole(Configuration.GetSection("Logging"));
loggerFactory.AddDebug();
//custom middleware
app.UseFlixOneLoggerMiddleware();
```

In the preceding code, we take advantage of `ILoggerFactory` and add `Console` and `Debug` to log the requests and responses. The `UseFlixOneLoggerMiddleware` method is actually an extension method. For this, add the following code to the `FlixOneStoreLoggerExtension` class:

```
public static class FlixOneStoreLoggerExtension
{
  public static IApplicationBuilder UseFlixOneLoggerMiddleware
  (this IApplicationBuilder applicationBuilder)
  {
    return applicationBuilder.UseMiddleware<FlixOneLoggerMiddleware>();
  }
}
```

Now, whenever any request comes to our product APIs, the log should appear, as shown in the following screenshot:

In this section, we created a custom middleware and then logged all requests and responses.

JSON-RPC for RPC communication

JSON-RPC is a stateless, lightweight remote procedure call (RPC) protocol. The specification (namely, JSON-RPC 2.0 specifications (see `http://www.jsonrpc.org/specification` for more details)) defines various data structures and their processing rules.

The main objects as per the specifications are shown in the following sections.

Request object

The `Request` object represents any call/request that is sent to the server. The `Request` object has the following members:

- **jsonrpc**: A string that indicates the version of the JSON-RPC protocol. It *must* be accurate (in this case, version 2.0).
- **method**: A string that has the name of the method to be adjured. Method names that begin with the word `rpc` and are succeeded by a period character (U+002E or ASCII 46) are restrained for rpc-internal methods and extensions, and *must not* be worn for anything else.

- **params**: A structured value that dominates the parameter values. It is to be worn throughout the conjuration of the method. This member *may* be deleted.
- **id**: An identifier fixed by the client that *must* have a string, number, or *null* value if constituted.

Response object

As per the specifications, whenever a call is made to the server, there must be a response from the server. The `Response` is expressed as a single JSON object with the following members:

- **jsonrpc**: A string that is the version of the JSON-RPC protocol
- **result**: A required member, if the request succeeds
- **error**: A required member, if there was an error
- **id**: A required member

In this section, we looked at an overview of JSON-RPC specification 2.0.

Summary

In this chapter, we discussed the integration of external APIs/components regarding payment gateways, order tracking, notification services, and so on. We also implemented their functionality by using actual code.

Testing is the one process that helps us to make our code error free. It is also a practice for all developers who want to make their code clean and maintainable. In the next chapter, we will cover the testing paradigm in day-to-day development activities. We will discuss some important terms associated with the test paradigm. We will also cover the theory around these terms, and then we will cover code examples, looking at stubs and mocks, and learning about integration, security, and performance testing.

Testing RESTful Web Services

6

A system cannot mature until it is tested in various scenarios. These scenarios are usually based on the experience of domain experts or existing production environments. There is always a chance that a system can crash in a production environment, even when the system is called a perfect system. For web applications, the conditions are even more critical due to performance glitches, bad user experience, and so on. A system should be put through a process or series of development principles to tackle these kinds of issues. Simply put, we must test the system. Testing is a process that ensures the quality of a system.

In other words, quality assurance, or testing, is a way to assess a system from different aspects. This process is also useful when a system requires testing to identify erroneous code, or if we want to assess its business compliance.

 Quality assurance is a process that assesses a system and ensures its quality.

Testing is entirely dependent on the architectural style of the system and it varies from system to system; everything depends on how we strategize our testing approach or plan.

In this chapter, we will mainly focus on testing RESTful services and making our code better by following the test-driven development approach. At the end of this chapter, you will be able to use the testing paradigm in day-to-day development activities with knowledge of stubs, mocks an understanding of integration and security, and performance testing.

In this chapter, we will cover the following topics:

- Test paradigms (the basics of quality assurance, including test case creation)
- Testing the ASP.NET core controller (unit testing)
- Stubs and mocking
- Security testing

- Integration testing
- Fake objects
- Testing service calls using Postman, Advanced RESTClient, and so on
- User acceptance testing
- Performance or load testing

Test paradigms

In the previous section, we saw that testing and quality assurance is one of the most important parts of the software development cycle. We should take steps to design a framework that tests the software, which is called a **test paradigm**.

A test paradigm is a framework of testing. It is based on the way one plans on implementing testing. In short, a test paradigm is a testing methodology.

A test method is where you decide how to create test cases, including what its language will be, how you will document the test cases, and so on. This also tells you how you are going to execute the test methods (for example, with black box testing).

A test method is an approach that tests or verifies the specific output on the basis of specific inputs, without knowing the internal functionality of a system.

Before we create test cases or develop a test paradigm or framework for testing, we need to get to grips with some important terminology.

Test coverage and code coverage

In general terms, coverage is what is covered and how you measure that coverage. From a developer's point of view, writing a unit test in test-driven development tells us how and what area of code is covered.

A measurement of code executed during testing is code coverage. A measurement of test cases executed during testing is test coverage.

The code is unit tested and it is proven that covered code is tested. In this code coverage, there would be many things that have been covered, namely, lines of code, functions, conditions, expressions, API resources, and so on.

For software testing terms, refer to `http://castb.org/wp-content/uploads/2014/05/istqb_glossary_of_testing_terms_v2.3.pdf`.

Test coverage and code coverage can also cover any of the following testing types:

- Unit testing
- Security testing
- Integration testing

In the upcoming sections, we will look at these tests in detail using code examples.

Tasks, scenarios, and use cases

When someone is working with a test paradigm, they should know the terms task, scenario, and use case. In this section, we will discuss these terms in detail:

- **Task**: A task is a generic word not only relevant to the software industry but to many others, too. This is an act or piece of work that needs to be completed. There will be different ways to complete the task, but the overall intention with a task is that it should be completed. In different areas, tasks have different purposes. In scrum development (`https://whatis.techtarget.com/definition/storyboard`), a storyboard or task board helps developers understand the work that needs to be completed.

The following diagram illustrates what we mean by a task:

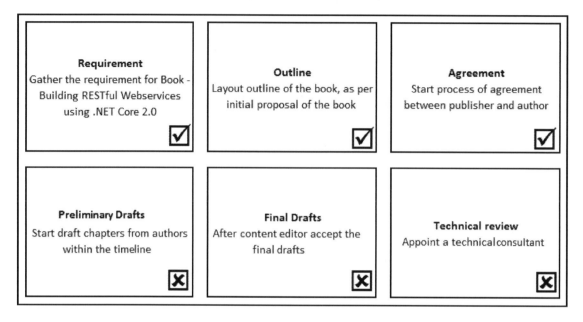

The preceding diagram is that of a story or task board; it displays the various tasks needed to finish a book, from data collection to the technical review. There are a lot of free or paid tools available on the market to manage these types of tasks.

- **Scenario**: Typically, a scenario is nothing but a situation where a system has failed after interaction with a customer. In other words, a scenario is a way of understanding and writing steps in detail. For example, there are a few situations that can cause a system's login functionality to fail, and these will be documented as a scenario. In software testing, scenarios are also known as test scenarios. A scenario usually leads to one or more tests.

- **Use case**: A use case is a set of possible sequences of interactions between a system and a user. It can also be a collection of possible scenarios that should be assessed when a system is implemented. These use cases are more detailed and documented, and are divided into various steps, as shown in the following flowchart:

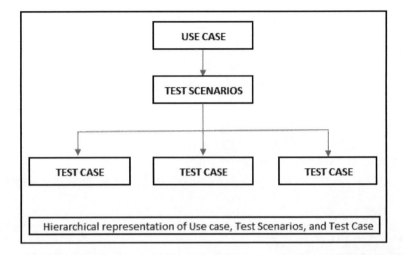

Hierarchical representation of Use case, Test Scenarios, and Test Case

In the preceding diagram, it is clear that **TEST CASE** is the sub-set of **TEST SCENARIOS**, and that **USE CASE** is the superset of **TEST SCENARIOS**. Whenever you create a test case, it comes down from a test scenario.

Checklist

In general, a checklist is nothing but a list of items, where an action is required in order to achieve a goal. A checklist could be a to-do list, a list of your day-to-day activities, or a list of a developer's tasks.

In the world of testing, a list could contain test cases to verify, a list of tests that need to be executed, and so on. A checklist varies from person to person, developer to developer, or even from organization to organization, but the purpose of a checklist is always to limit the very human behavior of forgetting something.

Bugs and defects

The terms bug and defect are the some of the most frequently used terms in the industry. In some organizations, these terms are used interchangeably. In general, however, a bug is related to something that is done correctly but executes an unexpected output, for example, 2 + 3 = 6. On the other hand, a defect is something that has been missed during planning.

Some things to note about bugs and defects:

- A bug is almost always due to the impure implementation of a requirement, for example, code that incorrectly fulfills a basic requirement
- Bugs are normally identified during development or in the testing phase
- A defect is related to a design or requirements gap that has slipped past a client or customer during production
- A defect often indicates human error
- Bugs can be fixed when caught during testing
- Defects can lead to a faulty system, which can lead to design issues

Testing approach

In general, a testing approach is an execution path illustrating how testing will be carried out. These approaches vary system to system; if one system requires a consultative approach, it does not mean that another system does. Different systems need different testing approaches.

A testing approach is a test strategy that is nothing but an implementation of a system or project.

Testing strategies should be clear to everyone so that the created tests can help non-technical members of the team (such as stakeholders) understand how the system is working. Such tests can be automated, such as testing the business flow, or they can be manual tests that can be performed by a user working on the User Acceptance Testing system.

Testing strategies or approaches have the following techniques:

- **Proactive**: This is a kind of early approach and tries to fix defects before the build is created from initial test designs
- **Reactive**: In this approach, testing is started once coding is complete

Test pyramid

The testing pyramid is a strategy or a way of defining what you should test in RESTful services. In other words, we can say a test pyramid helps us to define the testing scope of RESTful services.

 The concept of the testing pyramid was developed by Mike Cohn (`http://www.mountaingoatsoftware.com/blog/the-forgotten-layer-of-the-test-automation-pyramid`) in 2009.

There are various flavors of the testing pyramid; different authors have described this by indicating how they placed or prioritized their testing scope.

The following diagram depicts the same concept as defined by Mike Cohn:

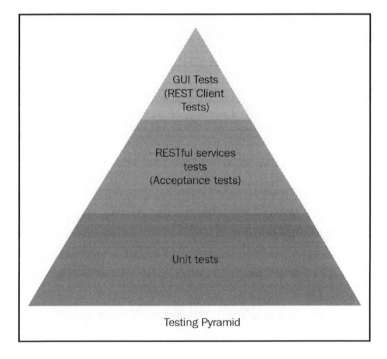

Let's talk about these layers in detail.

- **Unit tests**: These are tests that test small functionalities in units of an application of RESTful services developed in ASP.NET Core
- **RESTful service tests (Acceptance tests)**: These are tests that test an independent service or a service that communicates with another, often external, service
- **GUI tests (REST Client Tests)**: These tests belong to the client or consumer who will consume RESTful services; they help in testing an entire system with an aspect of the user interface and are end-to-end tests

 We will be discussing testing in respect to an application of a RESTful service developed in ASP.NET Core.

Types of tests

In the previous section, we discussed test approaches or testing strategies. These strategies decide how we will proceed with the testing of a system. In this section, we will discuss the various types of tests used in our application.

Testing the ASP.NET Core controller (unit testing)

Unit tests are tests that typically test a single function call to ensure that the smallest piece of the program is tested. So, these tests are meant to verify specific functionality without considering other components. Here, testing strategies come in handy and ensure that the best quality assurance of a system will be performed. It adds more power when it comes with the **test-driven development (TDD)** approach.

 You can learn and practice TDD with the help of Katas at `https://github.com/garora/TDD-Katas`.

We will discuss this with the help of a code example. Before we proceed further, please take a look at the following prerequisites:

- Visual Studio 2017 Update 3 or later
- .NET Core 2.0 or later
- C# 7.0 or later
- ASP.NET Core 2.0 or later
- Entity Framework Core 2.0 or later
- xUnit and MS tests
- The moq framework

Getting ready for the tests

In this section, we will create an ASP.NET Core API and then unit test it.

Complete the following steps to create your application:

1. Open Visual Studio.
2. **Go to File | New | Project** or press *Ctrl + Shift + F5*:

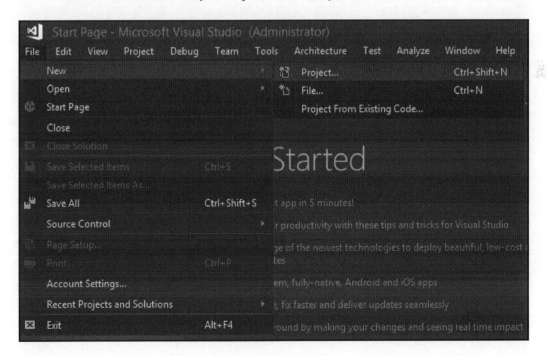

3. Select **ASP.NET Core Web Application.**

4. From the template window, select **ASP.NET Core API**—make sure you select **.NET Core 2.0.**

5. Name the project, choose the path for the solution, and click **OK.**

6. Add the `Core` folder—in **Solution Explore**, right-click and select **Add New Folder**, and name it `Model`.

7. Add the `Interfaces` and `Model` folders under the `Core` folder.

8. Add a new class under the `Model` folder—right-click on the `Model` folder in **Solution Explorer** and select **Add New Item**. Then, select **Class** or click *Shift + Alt + C.*

   Please note that the shortcut key varies as per your settings for Visual Studio.

9. Name it `Product.cs` and add the following code to this class:

```
namespace Chap06_01.Core.Model
{
  public class Product
  {
    public Guid Id { get; set; }
    public string Name { get; set; }
    public string Description { get; set; }
    public string Image { get; set; }
    public decimal Price { get; set; }
    public Guid CategoryId { get; set; }
    public virtual Category Category { get; set; }
  }
}
```

10. Repeat *steps 7* and *8* to add `Category.cs` and `ProductViewModel.cs`.

11. Repeat *step 6* and add the `Infrastructure` folder.

12. Add a new class under the `Infrastructure` folder—right-click on the `Infrastructure` folder in **Solution Explorer**, select **Add New Item**, and in that, select **Class** or click *Shift + Alt + C.*

13. Name it as `ProductContext.cs`.

   In this demo project, we are not following the test-driven development approach; we will unit test our application just for demonstration purposes.

14. Now, open the `appsettings.json` file and add the following code snippet:

```
"ConnectionStrings":
{
   "ProductConnection": "Data Source=.;Initial
   Catalog=ProductsDB;Integrated
   Security=True;MultipleActiveResultSets=True"
}
```

15. Right-click on **Project** in **Solution Explorer** and select **Manage Nuget Package.**

16. Under the **Nuget Package Manager** screen, search `Swashbuckle.AspNetCore` and install it.

> **Swagger** is open source and adheres to open specifications (`https://github.com/OAI/OpenAPI-Specification/blob/master/versions/2.0.md`). Swagger allows you to describe an API's structure. Swagger provides documentation to users (devs who are going to use APIs). There are a lot of open source and commercial tools available that can integrate with Swagger.
>
>
>
> **Swagger CodeGen** (`https://swagger.io/swagger-codegen/`) helps to generate client libraries for an API.
>
> **Swagger UI** (`https://swagger.io/swagger-ui/`) helps to generate an API's documentation.
>
> **Swashbuckle.AspNetCore** (`https://github.com/domaindrivendev/Swashbuckle.AspNetCore`) is a tool that helps document APIs built on ASP.NET Core.

17. Add `interface IProductRepository` under `Core/Interfaces`.

18. Add the following code to the `IProductRepository` interface:

```
namespace Chap06_01.Core.Interfaces
{
   public interface IProductRepository
   {
      void Add(Product product);
      IEnumerable<Product> GetAll();
      Product GetBy(Guid id);
      void Remove(Guid id);
      void Update(Product product);
   }
}
```

Please note that for the complete source code, refer to the GitHub repository at `https://github.com/PacktPublishing/Building-RESTful-Web-Services-with-DotNET-Core`.

19. Add the `ProductRepository` class under the `Infrastructure` folder.
20. Add the following code to `ProductRepository`:

```
namespace Chap06_01.Infrastructure
{
  public class ProductRepository : IProductRepository
  {
    private readonly ProductContext _context;
    public ProductRepository(ProductContext context)
    => _context = context;
    public IEnumerable<Product> GetAll() =>
    _context.Products.Include(c =>
    c.Category).ToList();
    public Product GetBy(Guid id) => _context.Products.
    Include(c => c.Category).FirstOrDefault(x => x.Id == id);
    public void Add(Product product)
    {
      _context.Products.Add(product);
      _context.SaveChanges();
    }
    public void Update(Product product)
    {
      _context.Update(product);
      _context.SaveChanges();
    }
    public void Remove(Guid id)
    {
      var product = GetBy(id);
      _context.Remove(product);
      _context.SaveChanges();
    }
  }
}
```

21. Open the `Startup.cs` file and add the following code:

```
services.AddScoped<IProductRepository, ProductRepository>();
services.AddDbContext<ProductContext>
(
  o => o.UseSqlServer(Configuration.GetConnectionString
  ("ProductConnection"))
);
```

```
services.AddSwaggerGen
(
  swagger =>
  {
    swagger.SwaggerDoc("v1", new Info { Title = "Product
    APIs", Version = "v1" });
  }
);
```

Your project hierarchy should now look like the following screenshot of **Solution Explorer**:

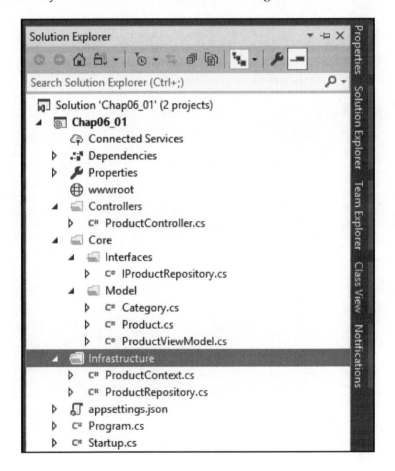

Now, you are ready to play with the application! Run the application from **Menu** or press *F5*. In a web browser, add the suffix /swagger to the URL in the address bar, as shown in the following screenshot:

This URL should show the swagger API documentation, as shown in the following screenshot:

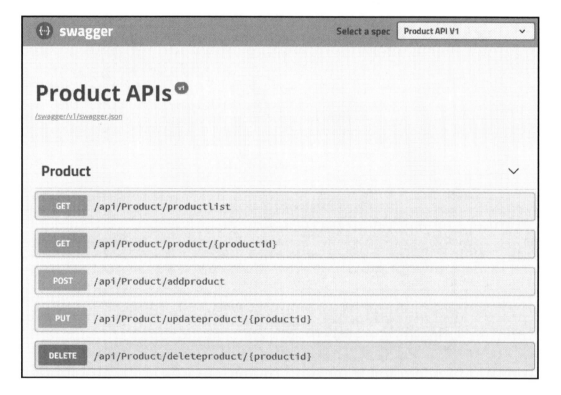

If you click on **GET /api/Product/productlist**, it should return a list of products, as shown in the following screenshot:

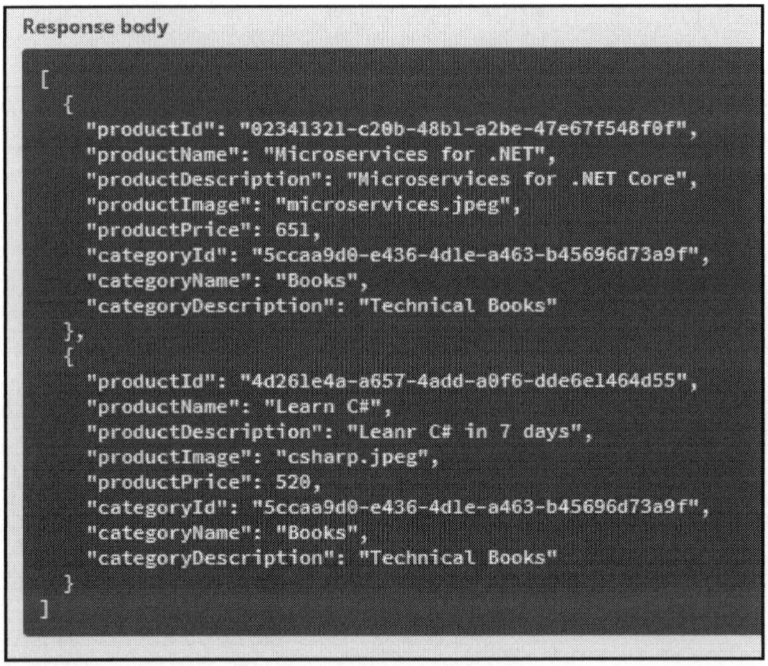

```
Response body

[
  {
    "productId": "02341321-c20b-48b1-a2be-47e67f548f0f",
    "productName": "Microservices for .NET",
    "productDescription": "Microservices for .NET Core",
    "productImage": "microservices.jpeg",
    "productPrice": 651,
    "categoryId": "5ccaa9d0-e436-4d1e-a463-b45696d73a9f",
    "categoryName": "Books",
    "categoryDescription": "Technical Books"
  },
  {
    "productId": "4d261e4a-a657-4add-a0f6-dde6e1464d55",
    "productName": "Learn C#",
    "productDescription": "Leanr C# in 7 days",
    "productImage": "csharp.jpeg",
    "productPrice": 520,
    "categoryId": "5ccaa9d0-e436-4d1e-a463-b45696d73a9f",
    "categoryName": "Books",
    "categoryDescription": "Technical Books"
  }
]
```

Writing unit tests

In this section, we will add a test project using ASP.NET Core 2.0 and write unit tests using xUnit. Before we start writing tests, we should set up a test project in our existing application.

The following are a few simple steps needed for our test project setup:

1. From **Solution Explorer** in Visual Studio, right-click on **Solution 'Chap06_01' (1 project)** and click on **Add | New Project...** , as shown in the following screenshot:

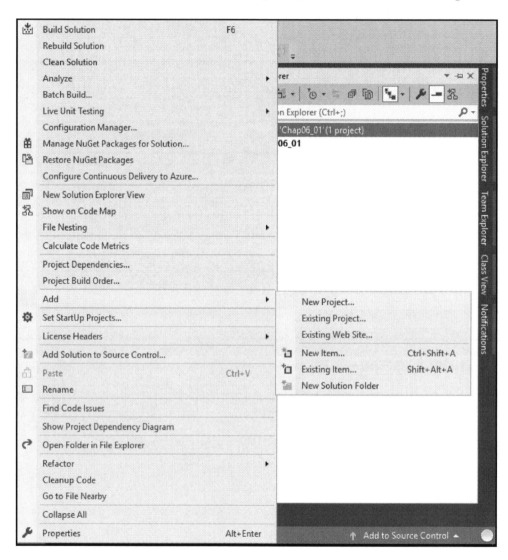

2. From the **Add New Project** template, select **.NET Core** and **xUnit Test Project (.NET Core)** and provide a meaningful name, for example, `Chap06_01_Test`:

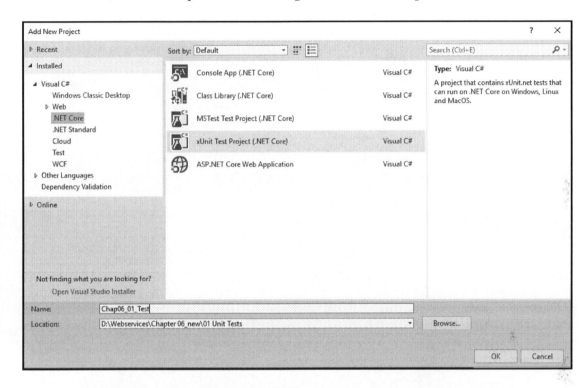

3. Add folders named `Fake` and `Services`. (Refer to the previous section to see how to add a new folder from the solution explorer.) Your project structure should now look like the following screenshot:

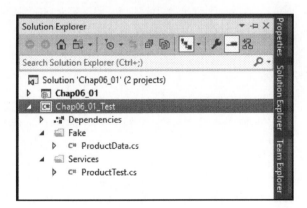

4. The `ProductData.cs` class should look like the following:

```csharp
namespace Chap06_01_Test.Fake
{
  public class ProductData
  {
    public IEnumerable<ProductViewModel> GetProducts()
    {
      var productVm = new List<ProductViewModel>
      {
        new ProductViewModel
        {
          CategoryId = Guid.NewGuid(),
          CategoryDescription = "Category Description",
          CategoryName = "Category Name",
          ProductDescription = "Product Description",
          ProductId = Guid.NewGuid(),
          ProductImage = "Image full path",
          ProductName = "Product Name",
          ProductPrice = 112M
        },
        new ProductViewModel
        {
          CategoryId = Guid.NewGuid(),
          CategoryDescription = "Category Description-01",
          CategoryName = "Category Name-01",
          ProductDescription = "Product Description-01",
          ProductId = Guid.NewGuid(),
          ProductImage = "Image full path",
          ProductName = "Product Name-01",
          ProductPrice = 12M
        }
      };
      return productVm;
    }
    public IEnumerable<Product> GetProductList()
    {
      return new List<Product>
      {
        new Product
        {
          Category = new Category(),
          CategoryId = Guid.NewGuid(),
          Description = "Product Description-01",
          Id = Guid.NewGuid(),
          Image = "image full path",
          Name = "Product Name-01",
```

```
            Price = 12M
        },
        new Product
        {
            Category = new Category(),
            CategoryId = Guid.NewGuid(),
            Description = "Product Description-02",
            Id = Guid.NewGuid(),
            Image = "image full path",
            Name = "Product Name-02",
            Price = 125M
        }
    };
    }
    }
}
```

In the preceding code snippet, we created fake data for `Products` and `ProductsViewModel`.

The full code is available to download from `https://github.com/ PacktPublishing/Building-RESTful-Web-Services-with-DotNET-Core`.

5. `ProductTest.cs`, our unit testing class, looks like the following:

Important terms for xUnit:

- **Fact** is an attribute and is used for a normal test method that is without parameters
- **Theory** is an attribute and is used for a parameterized test method

```
namespace Chap06_01_Test.Services
{
    public class ProductTests
    {
        [Fact]
        public void Get_Returns_ActionResults()
        {
            // Arrange
            var mockRepo = new Mock<IProductRepository>();
            mockRepo.Setup(repo => repo.GetAll()).Returns(new
            ProductData().GetProductList());
```

```
            var controller = new ProductController(mockRepo.Object);
            // Act
            var result = controller.GetList();
            // Assert
            var viewResult = Assert.IsType<OkObjectResult>(result);
            var model =
            Assert.IsAssignableFrom<IEnumerable<ProductViewModel>>
            (viewResult.Value);
            Assert.NotNull(model);
            Assert.Equal(2, model.Count());
        }
    }
}
```

In the preceding code snippet, we are simply testing our `ProductController`, which is a `Get` resource, `GetList`. In this code, we are mocking the list; we are not actually hitting the database but instead testing our `Controller` methods using fake data.

6. Run tests from **Test Explorer;** if your test passes, you should see something like the following screenshot:

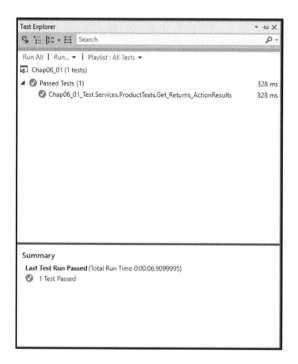

Stubs and mocking

Stubs are canned responses to calls made during a test, whereas mocks are meant to set expectations. They can be further explained as follows:

- **Stubs**: In the `stubs` object, we always get a valid stubbed response. The response doesn't care what input you provided. In any circumstance, the output will be the same.
- **Mocks**: In the `mock` object, we can test or validate methods that can be called on mocked objects. This is a fake object that validates whether a unit test failed or passed. In other words, we can say that mock objects are just replicas of our actual object.

In the previous section, *Writing unit tests*, we used the moq framework to implement the mocked objects.

Security testing

Security is a very wide-reaching term and can't be explained in a few lines. In general, security testing is a way of testing whether an application is secure or if there is any chance of leaking someone's data.

> Security and secure systems will be discussed in Chapter 8, *Securing RESTful Web Services*.

Security testing is very important, especially when we working in web-based applications. Web applications are publicly available and vulnerable to attack, so authentication and authorization are the most important factors here.

> FxCop (`https://en.wikipedia.org/wiki/FxCop`), which is shipped with Visual Studio and VeraCode (`https://www.veracode.com/`), is one of the most popular tools used in security testing.

Integration testing

In unit testing, we test a single unit of code, whereas, in integration testing in a Web API, we test all services that work together (internal and external, including third-party components). Service calls should be made to ensured integration with external services.

Run tests

Let's take the same application we created in the previous section for unit tests:

1. Add a new project for integration tests, and make sure the project structure looks like the following screenshot:

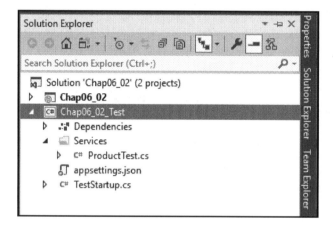

2. Write the following code in the constructor of `ProductTest.cs`:

```
var server = new TestServer
(
  new WebHostBuilder()
  .UseStartup<TestStartup>()
);
_client = server.CreateClient();
```

In the preceding code block, we initialized `TestServer`, where we used `TestStartup` as our startup entry file. Finally, we created a `private readonly HttpClient _client;` of our `WebHostBuilder()`.

3. Then, write a simple method that calls the **productlist** resource:

```
[Fact]
public async Task ReturnProductList()
{
  // Act
  var response = await _client.GetAsync("api/Product
  /productlist");
  response.EnsureSuccessStatusCode();
  var responseString = await response.Content.ReadAsStringAsync();
  // Assert
  Assert.NotEmpty(responseString);
}
```

In the preceding code, we are consuming our resource GET
`api/product/productlist` and testing it to see if it returns the expected
output.

To run the code smoothly, you need to add
the `Microsoft.AspNetCore.Hosting;` and
`Microsoft.AspNetCore.TestHost;` namespaces in the code.

This test also makes sure that the internal component, or any external service call
made by this method, is working as expected.

4. Complete the code for `ProductTes.cs` as follows:

```
namespace Chap06_02_Test.Services
{
  public class ProductTest
  {
    public ProductTest()
    {
      // Arrange
      var server = new TestServer(new WebHostBuilder()
      .UseStartup<TestStartup>());
      _client = server.CreateClient();
    }
    private readonly HttpClient _client;
    [Fact]
    public async Task ReturnProductList()
    {
      // Act
      var response = await
      _client.GetAsync("api/Product/productlist");
```

```
            response.EnsureSuccessStatusCode();
            var responseString = await
            response.Content.ReadAsStringAsync();
            // Assert
            Assert.NotEmpty(responseString);
        }
    }
}
```

5. Write the code for the TestStartup file as follows:

```
namespace Chap06_02_Test
{
    public class TestStartup : Startup
    {
        public TestStartup(IConfiguration configuration) :
        base(configuration)
        {  }
        public static IConfiguration InitConfiguration()
        {
            var config = new ConfigurationBuilder()
            .AddJsonFile("appsettings.json")
            .Build();
            return config;
        }
        public override void ConfigureServices(
        IServiceCollection services)
        {
            //mock context
            services.AddDbContext<ProductContext>
            (
                o => o.UseSqlServer
                (
                    InitConfiguration().GetConnectionString
                    (
                        "ProductConnection"
                    )
                )
            );
            services.AddMvc();
            services.AddScoped<IProductRepository,
            ProductRepository>();
        }
        public override void Configure
        (
            IApplicationBuilder app, IHostingEnvironment env
        )
        {
```

```
        app.UseStaticFiles();
        app.UseMvc();
    }
  }
}
```

In the preceding code, our `TestStartup` class inherited the `Startup` class, meaning we are now using its members and methods.

You need to make the methods `ConfigureServices` and `Configure` virtual to override these in the `TestStartup` class.

Take a look into our `InitConfiguration()` method; this method adds your test configuration file so that you can use test config values in any other environment.

In our `TestStartup` class, we overrode the `ConfigureServices` and `Configure` methods so that we could configure test services or any utilities class that was created specifically for testing purposes.

Now we are all set to run our tests, open **Test Explorer** and run a selected test. You can also run tests from the `ProductTest.cs` file (just right-click and select **Run tests**).

In case you need to debug the code, you can debug tests as well. If you do, you should get the following results:

You can write as many tests as you want. Tests also depend on what code you want to test.

Fake objects

As the name suggests, fake objects are objects that are not real. Fake objects are for testing purposes and contain actual code, but not with all of the genuine functionality. For instance, we can create a fake object to fetch data records using Entity Framework Core; in this case, we prefer to use InMemory (`https://docs.microsoft.com/en-us/ef/core/miscellaneous/testing/in-memory`) instead of a direct DB connection.

Run tests

Let's take the application we developed in the previous section on unit testing. Follow the steps mentioned in the preceding section and add a new xUnit test project.

We are looking for fake objects or data for testing purposes, so we will not be hitting our actual database server. Instead, here we will use the InMemory database.

 You need to add the `Microsoft.EntityFrameworkCore.InMemory` NuGet package to start the InMemory database.

We are not going to change anything here, but we will create fake data and records to test. To proceed, add the following code to the `TestStartup.cs` file in the `ConfigureServices` method:

```
//for tests use InMemory db
services.AddDbContext<ProductContext>
(
  o => o.UseInMemoryDatabase
  (
    InitConfiguration().GetConnectionString
    (
      "ProductConnection"
    )
  )
);
```

Here, we are using the following:

- The InMemory database, used only for testing purposes, by adding `.UseInMemoryDatabase` to the `TestStartup` class
- For our actual code, our database server will remain unchanged in the `Startup.cs` class, that is, `.UseSqlServer`

Now we need fake data and records, so add the following method in the `TestStartup` class:

```
private static void FakeData(DbContext context)
{
   var category = new Category
   {
      Id = ToGuid("A5DBF00D-2E29-4993-A0CA-7E861272C6DC"),
      Description = "Technical Videos",
      Name = "Videos"
   };
   context.Add(category);
   var product = new Product
   {
      Id = ToGuid("02341321-C20B-48B1-A2BE-47E67F548F0F"),
      CategoryId = category.Id,
      Description = "Microservices for .NET Core",
      Image = "microservices.jpeg",
      Name = "Microservices for .NET",
      Price = 651,
      InStock = 5
   };
   context.Add(product);
   context.SaveChanges();
}
```

Then, call the `FakeData(context)` method from the `Configure(IApplicationBuilder app, IHostingEnvironment env)` method, as shown in the following code:

```
public override void Configure(IApplicationBuilder app, IHostingEnvironment env)
{
    var context = app.ApplicationServices.GetService<ProductContext>();
    FakeData(context);
    app.UseStaticFiles();
    app.UseMvc();
}
```

Now we are ready to run tests, so open **Test Explorer** and hit **Run All**. If the tests pass, you should see something like the following screenshot:

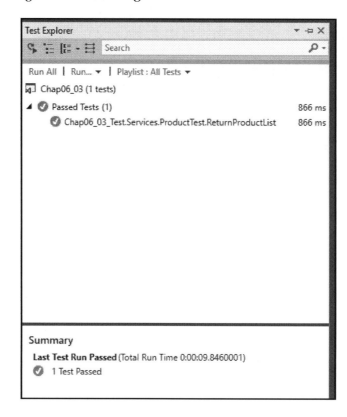

To double-check that the tests are not hitting the actual database, let's debug the test code. Open the `ProductTest.cs` class and set a breakpoint for the following test:

```
[Fact]
public async Task ReturnProductList()
{
  // Act
  var response = await _client.GetAsync("api/Product/productlist");
  response.EnsureSuccessStatusCode();
  var responseString = await response.Content.ReadAsStringAsync();
  // Assert
  Assert.NotEmpty(responseString);
}
```

Now right-click on **Debug Test**, use **step-into** (the *F11* key) to go into the controller and the repository, and check to see what the actual list of products is. You can see that our test is returning fake data, which means they are not hitting the actual database. The following is a screenshot of the debugged code:

```
2 references | 0 exceptions
private ProductViewModel ToProductvm(Product productModel)
    ≤ 2ms elapsed                                              productModel {Chap07_03.Core.Model.Product}
    return new ProductViewModel                            ▲  Category          {Chap07_03.Core.Model.Category}
    {                                                       ▶    Description  ٩ ▾ "Technical Videos"
        CategoryId = productModel.CategoryId,               ▶    Id               {a5dbf00d-2e29-4993-a0ca-7e861272c6dc}
        CategoryDescription = productModel.Category.Descr   ▶    Name         ٩ ▾ "Videos"
        CategoryName = productModel.Category.Name,          ▲  Products            Count = 1
        ProductDescription = productModel.Description,      ▲    [0]              {Chap07_03.Core.Model.Product}
        ProductId = productModel.Id,                        ▶      Category       {Chap07_03.Core.Model.Category}
        ProductImage = productModel.Image,                  ▶      CategoryId     {a5dbf00d-2e29-4993-a0ca-7e861272c6dc}
        ProductName = productModel.Name,                    ▶      Description  ٩ ▾ "Microservices for .NET Core"
        ProductPrice = productModel.Price                   ▶      Id             {02341321-c20b-48b1-a2be-47e67f548f0f}
    };                                                           Image        ٩ ▾ "microservices.jpeg"
                                                                 InStock        5
                                                                 Name         ٩ ▾ "Microservices for .NET"
                                                                 Price          651
```

The preceding screenshot is from a small application that we used to demonstrate testing with fake objects. With this testing approach, our fake objects were always hit instead of any actual code.

Testing service calls using Postman, Advanced REST Client, and more

There are a lot of tools available for testing RESTful web services and APIs. These tools provide the actual output.

 Web service testing tools are very useful when you have only API resources and want to test the expected output in different scenarios but do not have actual source code.

We will test our product APIs with the following two tools.

Postman

Postman (`https://www.getpostman.com/`) is one of the most popular tools when testing web service output. It also comes with a Google Chrome extension:

1. Launch Postman. If you don't have it, install it from the preceding link.
2. Select the **Resource type** as **GET** and enter the URL of the API; in our case, it is `http://localhost:60431/api/Product/productlist`.
3. Click on **Send** (alternatively, you can click on **Send and Download**, if you need data in the file).
4. If the test passes, you should see something like the following screenshot:

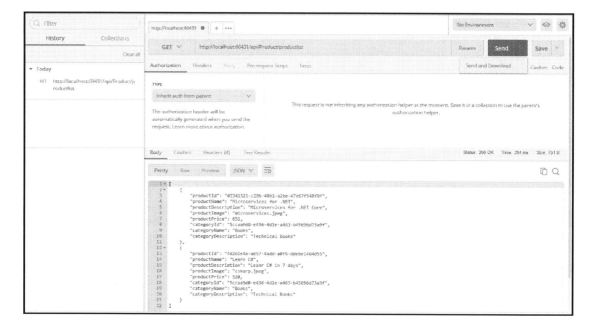

Advanced Rest Client

Advanced rest client (ARC) is another popular tool and also comes as a Chrome extension. You can either install it from the Chrome Extension store or directly from `https://install.advancedrestclient.com/`:

1. Install the Chrome extension for ARC, if not yet installed.
2. Launch ARC.
3. Pass the GET resource.
4. If the test passes, you should see something like the following screenshot:

User acceptance testing

As the name suggests, **user acceptance testing (UAT)** is testing that is done by users or accepted by users. In this testing methodology, users who might be an application's end user are involved directly with testing. There might be scenarios that users test in the production environment, or they may have access to the pre-tested results that they can accept or reject.

This kind of testing depends on the actual user who would be using the application in a production environment. This testing usually happens in a UAT or pre-production environment.

 The typical environments in the industry are known as development, staging, QA, UAT, pre-production, and production. In your organization, you might not have all the environments as per your project requirements; if so, refer to `https://www.guru99.com/user-acceptance-testing.html`.

UAT testing is also seen as final testing, and its acceptance or rejection tells us whether a current release will be deployed to production or not. The main focus of this testing is business-related. This testing does not deal with test code or the implementation of various patterns; it simply makes sure that all the business rules and requirements have been implemented.

Performance or load testing

For a web application's performance, scalability is very important. An application can be very secure, well tested, and created with good code but still be avoided by the user if it's not scalable.

 We will discuss scaling RESTful web services in detail in `Chapter 9`, *Scaling RESTful Services (Performance of Web Services)*.

Performance is very important for a good API, so we need to test and make sure that our application is able to load or stress large requests. Load testing is a non-functional type of testing (`https://www.guru99.com/non-functional-testing.html`) and the main aim of load testing is not to verify the code or test the code's health.

 The main purpose of this testing is to ensure that the web API is performing well based on various measures such as scalability, reliability, and so on.

The following are techniques or types of performance testing:

- **Load testing**: This tests the behavior of the system under various circumstances of specific load. This also covers critical transactions, database load, application servers, and so on.
- **Stress testing**: This is an approach where a system goes under regress testing and finds the upper-limit of a system's capacity. It is also determined by how a system behaves in a critical situation where the current load goes above the expected maximum load.
- **Soak testing**: This is also known as endurance testing. In this test, the main purpose is to monitor memory utilization, memory leaks, or various factors which affect system performance.
- **Spike testing**: This is an approach where we make sure that the system is able to sustain the workload. One of the best tasks for determining performance is suddenly increasing the user loads.

In ASP.NET Core, we can perform load testing with the help of the following:

- **Visual Studio**: If you have Visual Studio Enterprise Edition, you can easily create a load testing project; visit the following link for more information: `https://docs.microsoft.com/en-us/vsts/load-test`.
- **WebSurge**: This is a load testing use for APIs. You can use it in the cloud or for free for learning purposes. For more information, visit `http://websurge.west-wind.com/`.
- **BenchmarkDotNet**: This tool tells us how much of our code is performant. It tests different blocks of codes that give the same result to see which performs best. For more information, visit `https://github.com/dotnet/BenchmarkDotNet`.
- **Netling**: This is a load testing tool for web applications. With Netling, you can make changes and retest your code to meet your performance scale. For more information, visit `https://github.com/hallatore/Netling`.

 Explanations, along with working examples, of these tools and Visual Studio Load Testing is beyond the scope of this book.

In this section, we will simply test our product APIs to check how much time it takes them to list the products we request.

 You can also test the request time of APIs using a simple web client. In Chapter 10, *Building a Web Client (Consuming Web Services)*, we will discuss how to build a web client in detail.

Take a look at the code of our `ProductTest` class, as follows:

```
public class ProductTest
  {
    public ProductTest(ITestOutputHelper output)
    {
      _output = output;
    }
    private const double ExpectedRequestTime = 1000;
    private const int ApiLoad = 100;
    private const string RequestUri =
    "http://localhost:60431/api/product/productlist";
    private readonly ITestOutputHelper _output;
    private static double RequestCallTime()
    {
      DateTime start;
      DateTime end;
      using (var client = new HttpClient())
      {
        start = DateTime.Now;
        var response = client.GetAsync(RequestUri).Result;
        end = DateTime.Now
      }
      var actual = (end - start).TotalMilliseconds;
      return actual;
    }
    [Fact]
    public void SingleCallRequestTime()
    {
      var actual = RequestCallTime();
      _output.WriteLine($"Actual time: {ExpectedRequestTime}
      millisecond.
      Expected time: {actual} millisecond.");
      Assert.True(actual <= ExpectedRequestTime);
    }
    //code truncated
  }
```

The preceding code is self-explanatory. We are simply calculating the time taken by single and multiple requests, and checking whether this reaches our benchmark.

 The complete code is available to download from `https://github.com/ PacktPublishing/Building-RESTful-Web-Services-with-DotNET-Core`.

Run tests

To run tests, you need to make sure that your APIs are running and accessible using the URL. To do so, use the CLI to complete the following steps:

1. Open the Visual Studio command prompt
2. Locate the folder of your API project
3. Fire the command `dotnet run`

You should now a screen similar to the one in the following screenshot:

```
D:\Webservices\Chapter 06_new\04 Load Tests\Chap06_04>dotnet run
Using launch settings from D:\Webservices\Chapter 06_new\04 Load Tests\Chap06_04\Properties\launchSettings.json...
Hosting environment: Development
Content root path: D:\Webservices\Chapter 06_new\04 Load Tests\Chap06_04
Now listening on: http://localhost:60431
Application started. Press Ctrl+C to shut down.
```

Follow these steps to run tests using Visual Studio Test Explorer:

1. Open the `ProductTest.cs` file
2. Open Test Explorer
3. Click **Run**

This will run all the tests; you should see an output similar to the following screenshot:

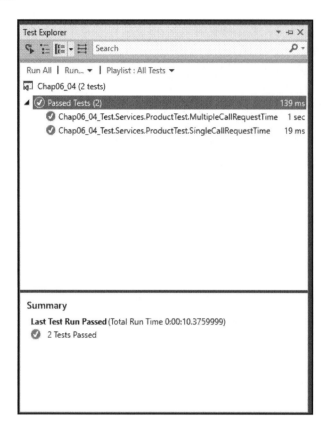

We can also check the exact time taken for a request to be completed by individual APIs. To do this, click on **Output** in the test explorer of a particular `TestCase` result, and you should see the following screen:

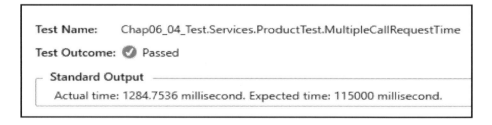

You can also run these tests using the CLI, as follows:

1. Open the Visual Studio command prompt
2. Locate the folder of your API project
3. Fire the command `dotnet test`

The preceding command will run all the tests; if they pass, you should see the following screen:

```
Test run for D:\Webservices\Chapter 06_new\04 Load Tests\Chap06_04_Test\bin\Debug\netcoreapp2
.0\Chap06_04_Test.dll(.NETCoreApp,Version=v2.0)
Microsoft (R) Test Execution Command Line Tool Version 15.6.0
Copyright (c) Microsoft Corporation.  All rights reserved.

Starting test execution, please wait...
[xUnit.net 00:00:01.0561900]   Discovering: Chap06_04_Test
[xUnit.net 00:00:01.2402047]   Discovered:  Chap06_04_Test
[xUnit.net 00:00:01.2468461]   Starting:    Chap06_04_Test
[xUnit.net 00:00:02.9754566]   Finished:    Chap06_04_Test

                         Total tests: 2. Passed: 2. Failed: 0. Skipped: 0.
Test Run Successful.
                         Test execution time: 5.6981 Seconds

               D:\Webservices\Chapter 06_new\04 Load Tests\Chap06_04_Test>
```

Visit `https://docs.microsoft.com/en-us/dotnet/core/tools/?tabs=netcore2x` to check all the available CLI commands.

In this section, we tried a simple load test that was based on request times. We tried a single call and multiple calls.

Summary

Testing helps to ensure our code is error-free. Testing is also a practice for all developers who want to make their code clean and maintainable. In this chapter, we covered testing paradigms in the day-to-day activities of a development team, with the knowledge of stubs and mocks, as well as the importance of understanding integration, security, and performance testing.

In the coming chapters, we will discuss security, including following the OWASP security standard and JWT authentication. We will cover more complex scenarios with the use of custom filters and input validations. Data protection is always a high priority for any web application, so we will also take a look at sensitive data persistence and storage.

7
Continuous Integration and Continuous Deployment

Most projects are a team effort. The team could be located in different places or in the same place, and members from different locations have to work in sync mode so their changes won't conflict with other team members. A system won't mature until it is used in various scenarios; these scenarios could be based on the experience of domain experts or come from the production environment. There is a chance that a system could crash in the production environment even if the system is regarded as a perfect system. In terms of web applications, the conditions are more critical due to performance glitches, bad user experiences, and so on. A system should go through a process where, if a team member makes changes, the code is integrated after unit tests and the build is then deployed in the related environment.

When we say deployment, Xcopy deployment immediately comes into our minds. In this type of deployment, you simply build and copy the related files and deploy/paste to a relevant environment.

In this chapter, we will discuss the fundamentals of deployment and the influence of emerging practices, such as **continuous integration (CI)** and **continuous deployment (CD)**. We will focus on the following topics:

- The Azure environment
- Publishing/hosting
- CI and CD using TFS online
- The difference between CI and CD

Introduction – deployment terminology

Before proceeding further, we should first discuss why we are talking about deployment. The deployment cycle is one that has a specific flow and we should understand the deployment terminology. Deployment terminology simply includes the steps that start with code changes up to release. In this section, we will discuss all these deployment steps.

The build stage

In the build stage, the service source gets compiled without any errors along with the passing of all corresponding unit tests. This stage produces build artifacts.

Continuous integration

CI forces the entire application to be built again every time a developer commits any change—the application code gets compiled and a comprehensive set of automated tests is run against it. This practice emerged from the problems of the frequent integration of code in large teams. The basic idea is to keep the delta, or change to the software, small. This provides confidence that the software is in a workable state. Even if a check-in made by a developer breaks the system, it is easy to fix it using this process.

Deployment

Hardware provisioning, installing the base OS and the correct version of the .NET framework are prerequisites for deployment. The next part of it is to advance these build artifacts into production through various stages. The combination of these two parts is referred to as the deployment stage. There is no distinction between the deployment and release stages in most of the applications.

Continuous deployment

In CD, each successful build gets deployed to a preferred environment, for example, production. Environments vary from organization to organization. So, CD is not meant for a production environment but you can use it for other environments too like dev, staging, and so on. CD is more important from a technical team's perspective. Under CD, there are several other practices, such as automated unit testing, labeling, versioning of build numbers, and traceability of changes. With continuous delivery, the technical team ensures that the changes pushed to production through various lower environments work as expected in production. Usually, these are small and deployed very quickly.

Continuous delivery

Continuous delivery is different from CD. CD comes from a technical team's perspective, whereas continuous delivery is more focused on providing the deployed code as early as possible to the customer. To make sure that customers get the right defect-free product, in continuous delivery, every build must pass through all the quality assurance checks. Once the product passes the satisfactory quality verification, it is the business stakeholders' decision when to release it.

Build and deployment pipeline

The build and deployment pipeline is part of implementing continuous delivery through automation. It is a workflow of steps through which the code is committed in the source repository. At the other end of the deployment pipeline, the artifacts for release are produced. Some of the steps that may make up the build and deployment pipeline are as follows:

- Unit tests
- Integration tests
- Code coverage and static analysis
- Regression tests
- Deployments to staging environment
- Load/stress tests
- Deployment to release repository

Release

A business feature made available to the end user is referred to as the release of a feature. To release a feature or service, the relevant build artifacts should be deployed beforehand. Usually, the feature toggle manages the release of a feature. If the feature flag (also called the feature toggle) is not switched on in production, it is called a dark release of the specified feature.

Prerequisites for successful RESTful services deployments

The success of any system deployment depends upon the architectural style and practices the team is following. Our RESTful services have more chances of being successful with the adoption of the following practices:

- **Self-sufficient teams**: Amazon, which is a pioneer of SOA and microservice architectures, follows the Two Pizza Teams paradigm. This means usually a microservice team will have no more than 7 – 10 team members. These team members will have all the necessary skills and roles; for example, development, operations, and business analyst. Such a service team handles the development, operations, and management of a microservice.
- **CI and CD**: CI and CD are prerequisites for implementing RESTful services that are a part of a system based on a microservices architectural style. Smaller self-sufficient teams, that can integrate their work frequently, are precursors to the success of microservices. This architecture is not as simple as a monolith. However, automation and the ability to push code upgrades regularly enables teams to handle complexity. Tools, such as **Team Foundation Online Services (TFS)**, TeamCity, and Jenkins, are quite popular toolchains in this space.
- **Infrastructure as code**: The idea of representing hardware and infrastructure components, such as networks with code, is new. It helps you make deployment environments, such as integration, testing, and production, look exactly identical. This means developers and test engineers will be able to reproduce production defects easily in lower environments. With tools such as CFEngine, Chef, Puppet, Ansible, and Powershell DSC, you can write your entire infrastructure as code. With this paradigm shift, you can also put your infrastructure under a version control system and ship it as an artifact in deployment.

- **Utilization of cloud-computing**: Cloud computing is a big catalyst for adopting microservices. It is not mandatory, as such, for microservice deployment though. Cloud computing comes with a near-infinite scale, elasticity, and rapid provisioning capability. It is a no-brainer that the cloud is a natural ally of microservices. So, knowledge and experience with the Azure cloud will help you adopt microservices.

The Azure environment

Azure is a Microsoft service that offers various cloud-computing services. Azure is a cloud platform that helps you to build, deploy, and manage applications globally.

Before we discuss the Azure environment, we should understand cloud-computing.

Cloud computing

In simple words, cloud-computing is a store/place that provides various computer-based services namely storage, databases, servers, and software, over the internet (here, the internet is termed as the cloud).

 There are various terms in existence related to cloud-computing, you can refer to this link for these terms: `https://azure.microsoft.com/en-in/overview/cloud-computing-dictionary/`.

These services can be sold by anyone and the vendors/companies that provide these cloud-computing services are called cloud providers.

Cloud-computing is not a new term, it has been around for a while, it's just that now it has become popular. If you are using any online services that help you to send or receive your emails to or from other persons, then this is cloud-computing. With the help of the cloud, you can do almost anything you want. These services include:

- Creation of new applications
- Storing data
- Hosting, deploying applications

And there are many more activities, depending upon the services offered by your cloud provider or what kind of subscription you have.

The benefits of the cloud

These days, cloud-computing plays an important role in the growth of businesses related to IT resources. Nowadays, everyone is thinking differently from a legacy system; the cloud has benefits for all with its advantages, as discussed here:

- **Pick and start**: If you have any type of subscription with cloud-computing you won't need to think, just pick your service and start from anywhere. You just require an internet to start with.
- **Cost**: When you go with the cloud, there is no need to think about spending money on buying costly hardware or related infrastructure. You can get the kinds of hardware you require and these are cost-effective.
- **Speed**: You can commission new resources quickly; these services are very performant.
- **Availability**: The most important benefit of cloud-computing is that you need not think about the availability of services as these are globally available. For example, if you commissioned a virtual machine from India then you need not worry about using this machine even though you may be in another part of the world.

 To decide what cloud provider suits you, refer to `https://azure.microsoft.com/en-in/overview/choosing-a-cloud-service-provider/`.

Cloud-computing service models

There is a huge list of cloud-computing services, but the best types of cloud-computing services are defined as the following (other types are based on these service types only):

- **Infrastructure as a Service (IaaS)**: This provides infrastructure, namely storage, virtual machines, and so on. For more info, go to `https://azure.microsoft.com/en-in/overview/what-is-iaas/`.

- **Platform as a Service (PaaS)**: This provides an on-demand environment for activities such as development or testing, or managing applications. For more info, go to `https://azure.microsoft.com/en-in/overview/what-is-paas/`.
- **Software as a Service (SaaS)**: This provides software applications on demand. There might be various subscription models from the cloud-computing provider under which you can subscribe to specific software applications. For more information, go to `https://azure.microsoft.com/en-in/overview/what-is-saas/`.

Discussing the Azure environment

The Azure environment provides a way of getting its various services using the internet. The following screenshot represents a typical overview of all cloud-computing service models:

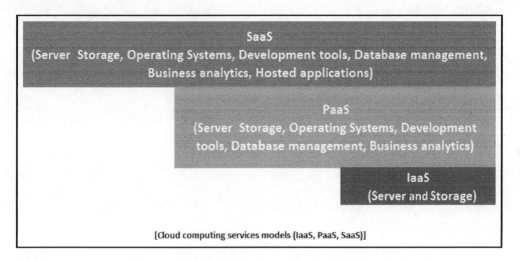

[Cloud computing services models (IaaS, PaaS, SaaS)]

It shows IaaS as a very basic model that provides servers and storage, and SaaS as the advanced model that provides almost all cloud-computing services.

Starting with Azure

To start with Azure, you need access to the Azure portal. Follow these steps:

1. Log in to the Azure portal using this link: `https://portal.azure.com`.

> If you don't have an account with Azure, create one for free here: `https:/ /azure.microsoft.com/en-in/free/`.

2. After login, you will see the dashboard as shown in the following screenshot:

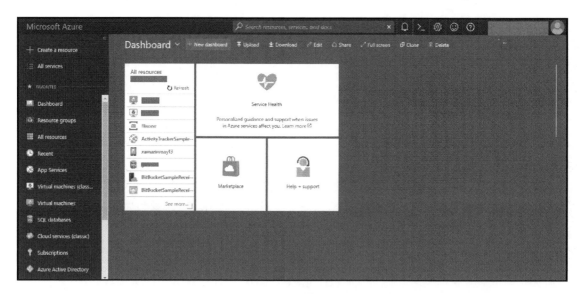

Azure portal dashboard

The portal dashboard may differ from what you saw in the preceding screenshot. If you logged in for the first time then you might need to create resources (as per your requirements). This is a place where you can commission your virtual machines (refer to IaaS), select a specific environment such as Windows machines or Linux (refer to PaaS), or you can deploy your applications (refer to SaaS).

3. Now you can do whatever you want to do as per your subscription.

Publishing/hosting

Publishing/hosting is a service that makes your application publicly available. Applications can be stored on servers provided by your hosting provider. In this section, we will use TFS (now VSTS): refer to `https://www.visualstudio.com/tfs/`.

> You need to migrate your existing project if it is hosted on TFS. Refer to the link for more details: `https://www.visualstudio.com/team-services/migrate-tfs-vsts/`.

Project hosting

You need to have access to Visual Studio Online/TFS Online (now VSTS) to host a project. For this you need to follow these steps:

1. Go to `https://www.visualstudio.com/vso/` using your preferred browser.
2. Click on **Sign in,** as shown:

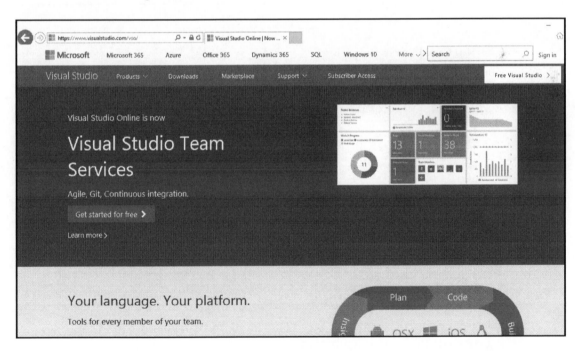

VSTS home screen

3. Enter your Microsoft account; you can create one if you don't have one.
4. Follow the steps and create your account.
5. You will be redirected to your **Visual Studio Team Services Accounts** page:

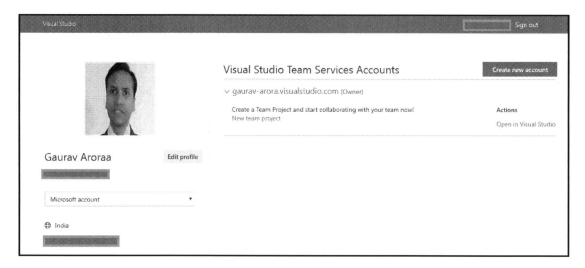

VSTS my profile page

6. Click on **Create new project.**
7. You will be redirected to a new page where you will be asked for some information related to your project.
8. Add your project information, as in the following screenshot:

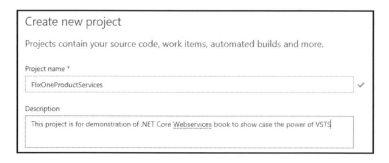

Creating a new project

9. Select your version control – you will be given the choice of **Git** or **Team Foundation Version Control (TFVC)**.

If you are confused with the options, refer to this link for a comparison between Git and TFVC: `https://docs.microsoft.com/en-us/vsts/tfvc/comparison-git-tfvc?view=vsts`.

In our case, select **Team Foundation Version Control**:

10. Now, select **Work Item Process**, refer to `https://docs.microsoft.com/en-us/vsts/work/work-items/guidance/choose-process?view=vsts` to know more about the various options available. In our case, select **Scrum**:

11. Now click on **Create**.

12. You will be redirected to a newly created project page that looks like the following screenshot:

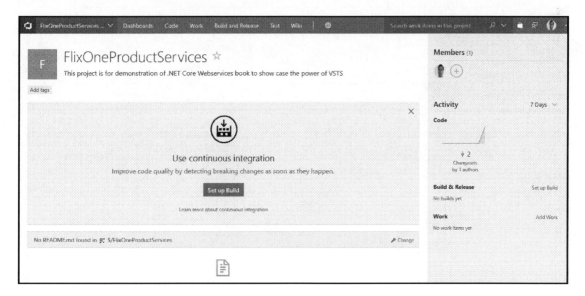

FlixOneProductServices project main screen

13. The project main screen is a quick display page, where you can see all the activities quickly.

Your project is created and now you are ready to start with your project.

The dashboard

The dashboard is a screen containing a snapshot of your project activities. It tells you what task is assigned to you, displays a sprint burndown chart, project progress, or whatever you've configured for your dashboard:

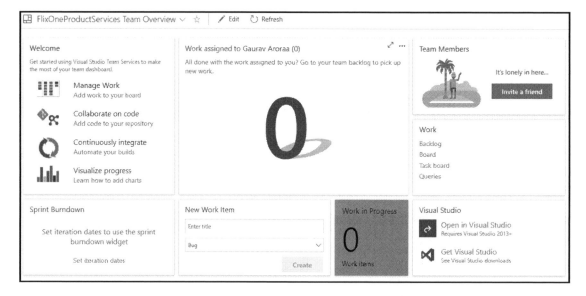

Dashboard of FlixOneProductServices project

From the project dashboard, you can edit your widget by adding new or removing existing widgets. The preceding screenshot shows the default view of our project.

Code

The following is the screen where you can manage your actual code for the current project:

Code screen of FlixOneProductServices project

You can view the following:

- **Files**: All the files in the repository.
- **Changeset**: Code changes with a changeset number, you can also get the information on what changeset pushed against what tasks/bugs.
- **Shelvesets**: Any shelve changes that are available for review or any other purpose related to the current project.
- **Pull Requests**: This is a way to work in a collaborative manner. You can initiate a **Pull Request** anytime, click on **Code** and select **New Pull Request,** and the owner or maintainers of the project will be notified about this pull request.

Work

By default, it displays the **Work Items** screen, showing you the items assigned to you or the tasks/bugs you're working on or have worked on. We have created a new project so you will get a blank page; to start with work items, you need to create a few backlog items and then assign them within the team.

Click on **Backlog** and then add a title for your **Product backlog** from the new template that appears on the screen. See the following screenshot:

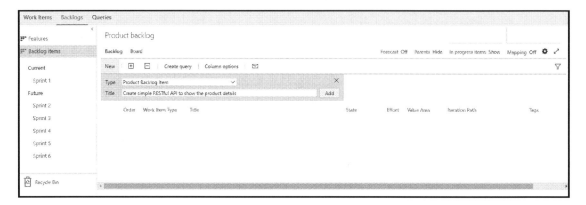

New product backlog

You can see in the preceding screenshot that, by default, you are given six sprints. Now, open a newly created product backlog item and provide a complete description – details such as efforts for this work, who will work on this item, or who will be the owner of this work item. See the following screenshot, which shows everything:

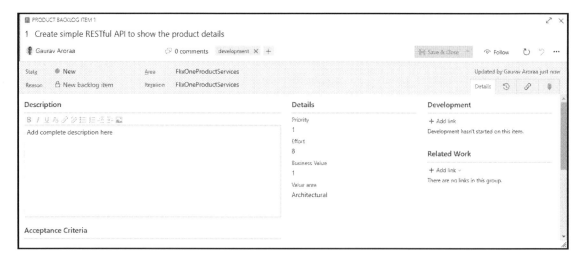

Product backlog item

Now, go to **Sprint 1** and set the dates – you should set the dates to start your current iteration as shown in the following screenshot:

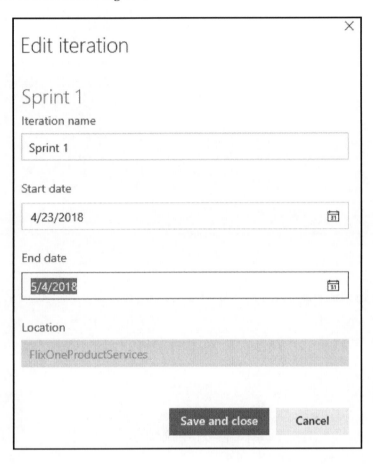

Similarly, you can add more product backlog items. Do not move items to **Sprint 1**. The board view of the **Backlog items** screen would look like the following screenshot:

Board backlog items

Adding code to the repository

We did not add any code to our repository; now, it's time to do that. To add code, you can either click on **Code** and upload the files directly from the web interface or go to **Source Control** from your Visual Studio IDE and check in the code after adding the repository. In this section, we will add our code using Visual Studio. To do so follow these steps:

1. Open Visual Studio
2. Create or open your existing project
3. Open Team Explorer
4. Click on **Connect TFS server**
5. Add a TFS server if you can't find a server, and then provide a valid address for it
6. Click **Connect**

The following screenshot shows a connection with FlixOneProductServices:

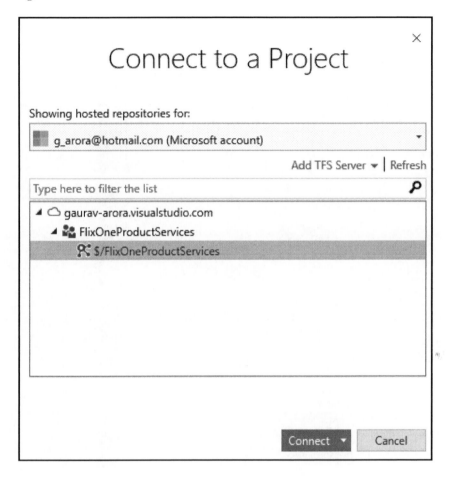

Connecting TFS server

7. You will need to map the TFS repository to your local drive. Map the source and get the code:

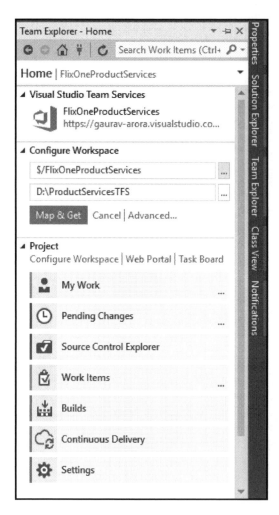

Mapping and getting source code

8. Now click on **Source Control Explorer** and the **Source Control Explorer** tab will be opened. You will see empty project nodes, as in the following screenshot:

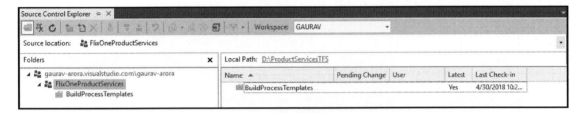

Source Control Explorer

9. From **Solution Control Explorer,** right-click on **Solution** and click on **Add Solution** to **Source Control.** Refer to the following screenshot:

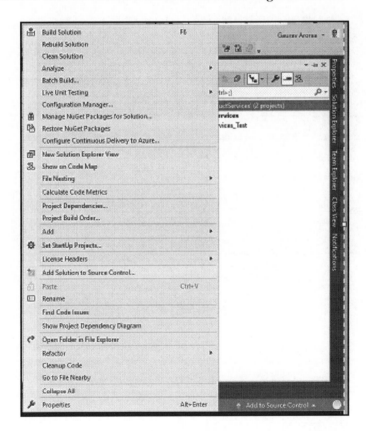

Add solution to Source Control

10. Make your choice and select it:

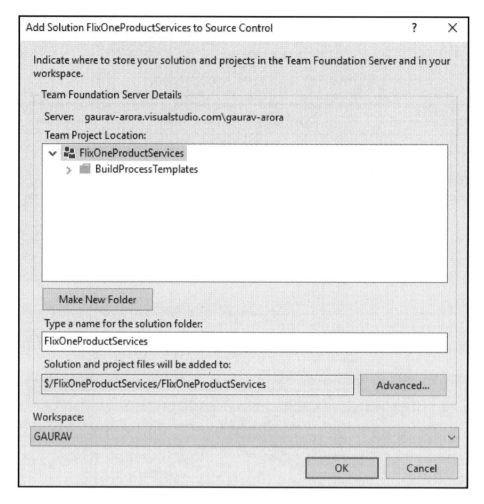

Add solution to FlixOneProductServices

11. Now you can see a new folder and files have been added into the **Source Control** – see the following screenshot:

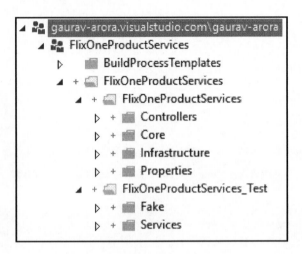

Newly added project

12. Go to **Team Explorer** and click on **Pending Changes**. You will find various files that are checked out.

13. Add a work item and add a comment and click on **Check In:**

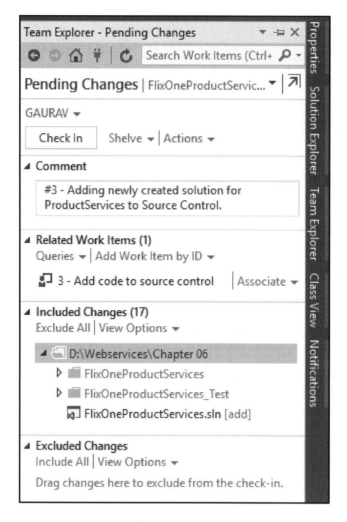

Check In pending changes

14. You have successfully added your solution to **Source Control.**

15. Now go back to your TFS Online and click on **Code**. You will find all the code files/folders recently added to **Source Control**. Refer to the following screenshot:

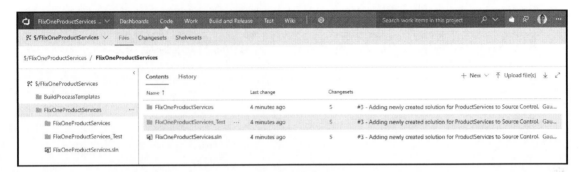

Viewing Code

You have successfully hosted your project to VSTS. In the following sections, we will discuss build and deployment.

Test

This screen of VSTS helps you to create various test plans so you can track manual testing for a sprint. It helps to monitor when manual testing is completed for the current sprint. We discussed various terms of testing in Chapter 6, *Testing RESTful Web Services*.

In the following sections, we will see how this helps us to test our sprint by creating a test plan and test cases.

Creating a test plan

From the **Test Plans** tab, click on + and then click on **Test plan,** as shown in the following screenshot:

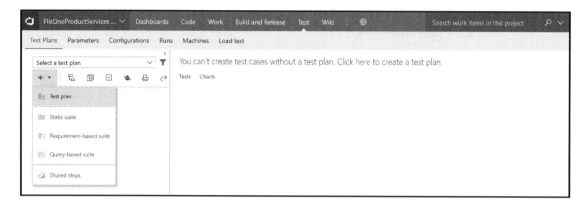

Creating a test plan

In the next screen, name your **Test plan,** make sure you have selected a correct sprint for the test plan. Refer to the following screenshot:

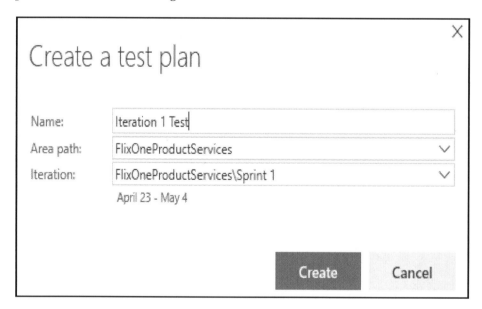

Naming your test plan

As the test plan is for a manual test, we now have to add the backlog items that need to be tested. In your case, we are just adding Sprint 1 backlog items. In doing this, we have added test suites for all backlog items of Sprint 1.

Creating test cases

In the previous section, we have created the **Iteration 1 Test plan** and added a test suite to it. Now, we need to create a test case, click on **New** and select **New test case**:

Creating a new test case

Complete your test case by adding a valid name, and the steps with expected output to the test case. Refer to the following screenshot:

Writing a test case

You can now assign the testers to these test cases or test suites so that testers can run these tests.

Running manual tests

In previous sections, we have created test cases that run manually. Click on the test suites and click on **Run** to run the available tests. Refer to the following screenshot:

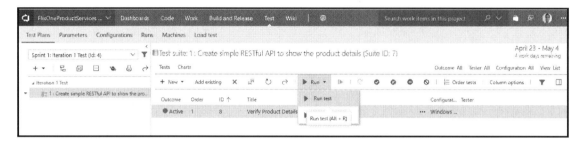

Running manual tests

These tests will run in the browser window so please make sure your browser doesn't block popups, as shown in the following screenshot:

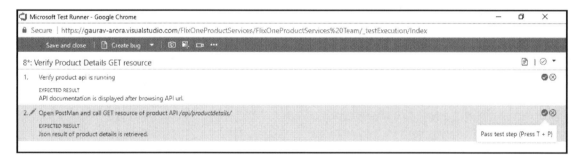

Verifying manual test results

As these tests are manual, you need to test these manually. After execution of these tests, you have to verify the expected output and mark the test as a pass or fail, accordingly. The overall results of test cases will be shown in the test suite window.

In this section, you have created a test plan, a test suite for the current iteration, and manual test cases to test a specific iteration, code changes, a build, or release.

Wiki

Wiki pages help team members to work together. These pages can consist of project documentation or instructions to work on a project such as coding guidelines, and so on. Initially, you will get a blank template by clicking the **Create Wiki** button, as shown in the following screenshot:

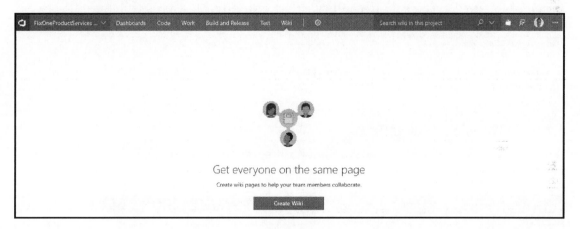

Creating Wiki

From the **Create Wiki** page template you can add as many pages as you want. Wiki pages support for markdown: https://docs.microsoft.com/en-us/vsts/collaborate/markdown-guidance?view=vsts.

Build and Release tab

The **Build and Release** tab provides the facility to create a build and release for the project. In this section, we will discuss CI and CD using VSTS. Initially, there would not be any build definition.

CI versus CD

We have already discussed these two methods in previous sections. In this section, we will briefly discuss the difference between CI and CD.

CI is a practice where by all team members (developers) integrate their code. This happens on every check-in, whenever a developer pushes changes, or as the code is configured, CI triggers. The most important advantage of this is that it saves time during your development cycle as it identifies conflicts, if there are any. This starts with the initial steps to set up automotive tests. As soon as someone pushes changes to the repository, it triggers the build and tests.

Continuous deployment solves the deployment problems of the code while deploying to the production environment.

CI and CD using TFS online

In this section, we will discuss the continuous integration of our project. Go to the **Builds** tab and then **Build Definitions** and click on **+ New**:

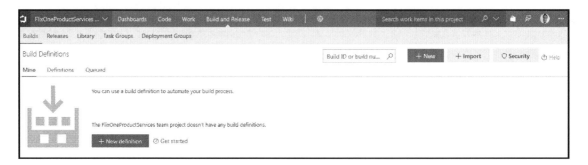

Creating a new definition

In the next step, the system will ask you to choose your repository. Select **Repository Source Control** and map the branches, then click on **Continue**:

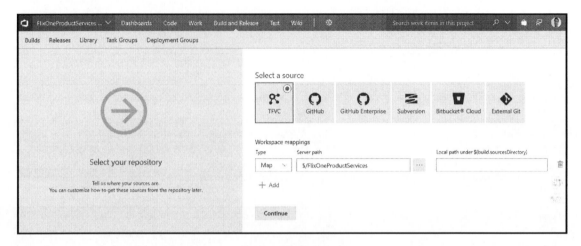

Selecting a repository source

From the next screen, choose your template; in our case, choose **ASP.NET Core**:

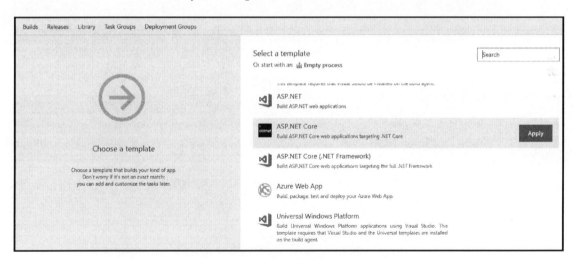

Selecting ASP.NET Core template

Follow the template instructions and provide the required values, as shown in the following screenshot:

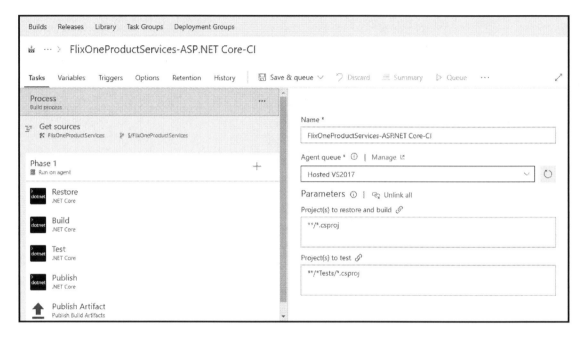

Creating build tasks

The following are the basic but important concepts related to VSTS; these are also important to understand so that you can configure build steps successfully:

- **Tasks**: These are the build steps that instruct VSTS to perform specific tasks
- **Variables**: These are the build configuration values that tell the build agent about system or custom values
- **Triggers**: These enable various tasks based on whether you have enabled CI or not
- **Options**: These are the build properties, for which you can provide build description, build job time out, and so on
- **Retention**: Retention policies can be built as required; typical policies are how long you want to keep good or bad builds with you

To make our example simple, I selected **Changeset #5** to save the build definition:

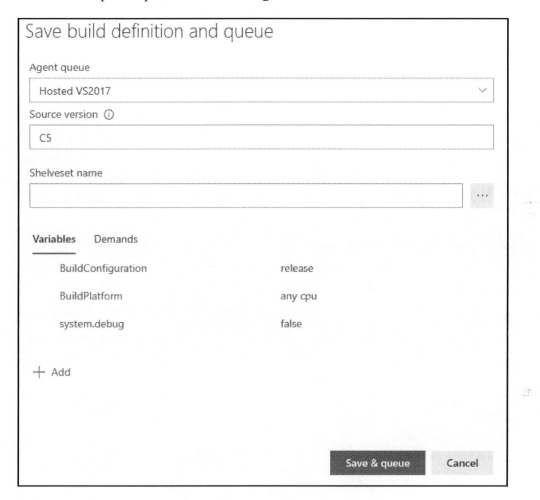

Saving build definition and queue

Now, you can see the build results under the **Build and Release** tab – your build might not be run (please revisit all the steps); the following screenshot shows the verified steps:

Build steps

Initiating the CD release process

You have already set up the CI process and now it's time to go with CD. Go to the **Release** tab and click on the **New definition** button:

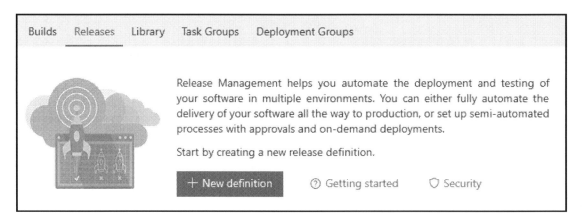

Adding release definition

Select a template as per your application. Refer to the following screenshot:

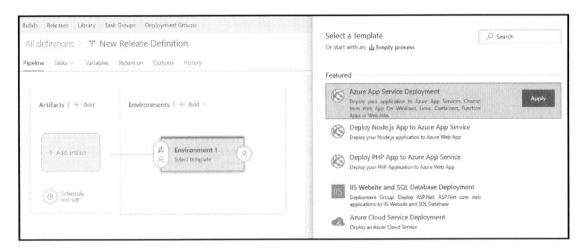

Selecting Azure App Service Deployment

Add an artifact to the release definition by selecting your repository or build, refer to the following screenshot:

Adding an artifact

Set values for your deployment environment, what Azure service, or app type you are going to use, and so on. Refer to the following screenshot:

Adding task values

Go to **Release** and you can see the status of your releases; we have added only one release definition so you will see something like the following screenshot:

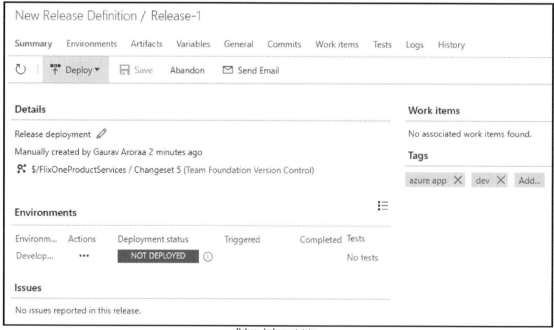

Release deployment status

We have not deployed our release yet so its status is **NOT DEPLOYED**. You can manually trigger the deployment. This release is meant for a development environment – you can set as many environments as you want. In this section, we have seen how to initiate CI and CD using VSTS.

Summary

Deployment terminology makes a team become aligned with its work, even if teams are working in different geographical zones. With the help of CI, CD teams are in sync as they receive recent changes immediately after check-ins by any of the teams working on the project.

In the next chapter, we will cover a testing paradigm in the day-to-day activities of development. We will discuss important terms associated with the test paradigm, including the theory around these terms, and then we will discuss code examples with a knowledge of Stubs, Mocks, and understanding integration and security, and performance testing.

8
Securing RESTful Web Services

In the world of web applications, where there are numerous request and response exchanges over HTTP, security is one of the most important cross-cutting concerns. Any unsecured service or web application can face datatampering issues.

"Whenever data is modified (destroyed, manipulated, or edited) by an unauthorized channel, it is generally called data tempering."

Data can be tampered with when it is in transit or in another place. There might be several reasons why data is tampered with—unprotected data is the most common reason in the industry. To prevent such issues, you can protect your environment and application systems. Generally, a firewall is the best way to protect your environment (server). You can protect an application by implementing an authorization mechanism.

Unfortunately, data breaches of well-known sites are commonplace these days. Taking this into account, information and application security has become critical to web applications. For the same reason, secure applications should no longer be an afterthought. Security is everyone's responsibility in an organization.

In this chapter, we will mainly be focused on security and the REST and OWASP security standards. By the end of this chapter, you will understand the concepts of authentication, single sign-on (SSO), token-based authentication, and authentication using a proxy server (such as Azure API Management). We will cover the following topics:

- OWASP standards for web security
- Securing RESTful web services
- Authentication and authorization
- Validations
- Data encryption and storing sensitive data

OWASP security standards

The **Open Web Application Security Project (OWASP)** is an online community that mainly works on web application security problems by creating various studies and standards. In this chapter, we will follow the security standards of OWASP that were released in 2017 (`https://www.owasp.org/index.php/Top_10-2017_Top_10`):

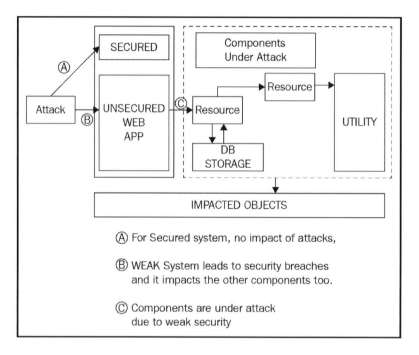

Application security risks

The preceding diagram is a pictorial overview of an application's security risks. It depicts how an attacker might attack a weaker application. The attacker attacks application components by injecting scripts (mostly JavaScript) and impacting the system. In this image, you will notice that only an unsecured portion of the web application is under attack. A secure system is safe, even after it has been attacked.

The following are application security risks as defined by OWASP:

- Injection
- Broken authentication
- Sensitive data exposure
- XML external entities (XXE)
- Broken access control
- Security misconfiguration
- Cross-site scripting (XSS)
- Insecure deserialization

These are high-alarmed security risks that should be handled in every web application.

Securing RESTful web services

Before you start with learning about securing RESTful web services, I would like to tell you about security in the world of the web. In general, the phrase *security* describes the measures that are taken to make sure that everything is secure. But what does *everything* include here? Let's elaborate: security is a way or a process that stops unauthenticated and unauthorized access to confidential data over web applications.

 The type of confidential data depends upon the nature of the web application—for example, if the web application is for medical and clinical services, then the confidential information consists of all the patients' data related to their tests, medical history, and so on.

The first step towards the creation of a security process is to authenticate and authorize access to the web application. If the request is not authenticated, then it should not be accepted by the system. It should also not be accepted if the request is authenticated, but not authorized to access the data of the web application.

The following diagram shows an overview of the authentication process, using Auth services:

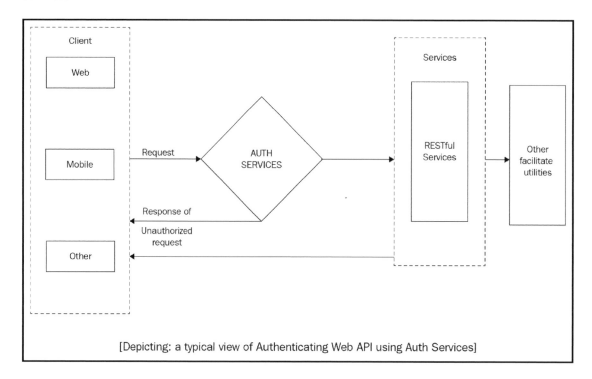

[Depicting: a typical view of Authenticating Web API using Auth Services]

In the preceding diagram, you can think about a typical ASP.NET Core API system that uses Auth services as a middleware server. There may be several clients or consumers who are using these services and can request access to the data. Here, Auth services play an important role in authenticating incoming requests from clients. If the Auth service identifies the request as authenticated, it generates a token and sends it to the API servers for further processing. If the request is not an authenticated request, then the Auth service notifies the client of the failed authentication. The preceding image is just an overview of a typical scenario. An actual scenario could be more complex, with the use of one or more middleware backend servers (typical API management servers).

In the following sections, you will get a better idea of the following two important security concepts:

- **Authentication**: Authentication is nothing but a process where a system verifies or identifies the incoming requests by some sort of credentials (generally a user ID and password). If the system finds that the provided credentials are wrong, then it notifies the user (generally via a message on the GUI screen) and terminates the authorization process.
- **Authorization**: Authorization always comes after authentication. It is a process that allows the authenticated user who raised the request to access resources or data after verifying they have access to the specific resources or data.

From this, you can conclude that the security of RESTful services is the most important feature of the application.

How can you maintain sessions in RESTful web services?
RESTful web services work with the HTTP protocol, which is a stateless protocol (`https://stackoverflow.com/questions/13200152/why-say-that-http-is-a-stateless-protocol`), and treat every request as a new request. There is no way in which the HTPP protocol helps to maintain sessions in RESTful web services. But, we can achieve this programmatically with the help of authenticated tokens. This technique is known as token-based authorization (we will discuss it in detail in the coming sections). With the help of this technique, you can authorize an authenticated user to allow data or resources for a predefined period of time.

Every request that comes via services or any other mode should be authenticated and authorized before the system responds to the user or the client that made the call. This process mainly includes the following:

- **Confidentiality**: The secured system makes sure that any sensitive data is not exposed to unauthenticated and unauthorized access requests
- **Availability**: The security measures in the system make sure that the system is available for users who are genuine, as confirmed through the system's authentication and authorization mechanism
- **Integrity**: In a secured system, data tampering is not possible, so the data is secure

The vulnerable areas of an unsecured web application

In today's web applications, the main vulnerable assets to protect from unauthorized access are the resources and data. If a site is unsecured, then the chances of vulnerability are high. According to the official website at `https://docs.microsoft.com/en-us/aspnet/core/security/`, the following areas are the main threats to any unsecured web application.

Cross-site scripting attacks

Cross-site scripting attacks—or XSS attacks—typically happen as a result of bad input, where an attacker injects client scripts (JavaScript in most cases) into the web page. According to the official web page (`https://docs.microsoft.com/en-us/aspnet/core/security/cross-site-scripting`):

> *"Cross-Site Scripting (XSS) is a security vulnerability which enables an attacker to place client-side scripts (usually JavaScript) into web pages."*

Here, I am using the example of a web client that consumes web services. You will learn more about web clients in `Chapter 10`, *Building a Web Client (Consuming Web Services)*.

The following screenshot shows a scenario where the **Create** screen is under attack:

The preceding screenshot is a representation of an unsecure web application. Here, the user can inject the script tag, and when the user clicks on **Create**, it is posted back to the server.

The following screenshot shows the code's debug mode, where we can see that our system is accepting script data:

The preceding screenshot shows how it was posted to the server and was eventually saved in the database or any persistent repository.

The following screenshot shows the affected page:

Whenever anyone accesses a page with affected data, it will show an alert, as shown in the preceding screenshot.

You can build a system that stops such attacks by applying a few code changes. I will cover this in the *Validations* section.

SQL injection attacks

An SQL injection attack is one of the most severe attacks that directly target the database. This is first in the list of OWASP application security risks. Attackers can steal a system's secured data with the help of SQL injection.

The following diagram shows the process of SQL injection:

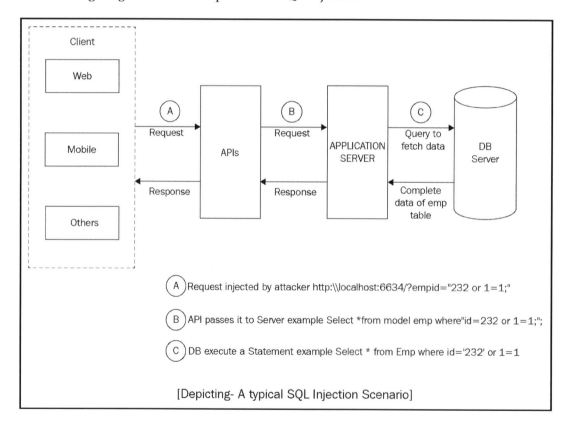

[Depicting- A typical SQL Injection Scenario]

In the preceding diagram, you can see a typical SQL injection scenario where the attacker has injected an `or` clause to fetch all of the data of a particular table. The actual code instruction was to return a single record based on the `EmpId` from the employee table. But as it was injected with an extra phrase, it returns the complete records of the employee table. This is the biggest problem with an unsecured system. Here, the attacker injected a simple clause into the statement.

What is cooking here?

In the previous section, you saw an imaginary scenario and went through an SQL injection in action. Let's look at an actual example by creating a RESTful product API using ASP.NET Core 2.0. Before you start building this application, bear in mind the following prerequisites for this application:

- Visual Studio 2017 update 3 or later
- ASP.NET Core 2.0 or later
- C#7.0 or later
- Microsoft Entity Framework Core 2.0.0

Go through the following steps to create our application:

1. Open Visual Studio.
2. Select **File | New | Project** or press *Ctrl + Shift + F5*.
3. Select **ASP.NET Core Web Application**.
4. From the template window, select **ASP.NET Core API**. Make sure you select **.NET Core 2.0**.
5. Name the project, choose the path for the solution, and click **OK**.
6. Add the `Models` folder. In **Solution Explore**, right-click, select **Add New Folder** from the drop-down menu, and name it `Models`.
7. Add a new class under the `Models` folder. Right-click on the `Models` folder in **Solution Explorer** and select **Add New Item | Class** from the drop-down menu, or use *Shift + Alt + C*.

> Please note that the shortcut keys vary as per your settings for Visual Studio.

8. Name it `Product.cs`, and add the following code to this class:

```
namespace Chap08_02.Models
{
  public class Product
  {
    public Guid Id { get; set; }
    public string Name { get; set; }
    public string Description { get; set; }
    public string Image { get; set; }
    public decimal Price { get; set; }
    public Guid CategoryId { get; set; }
    public virtual Category Category { get; set; }
  }
}
```

9. Repeat steps 7 and 8, adding `Category.cs` and `ProductViewModel.cs`.

10. Repeat step 6, adding the `Contexts` folder.

11. Add a new class under the `Contexts` folder. Right-click on the `Contexts` folder in **Solution Explorer**, select **Add New Item**, and in the dialog box, select **Class**, or use *Shift + Alt + C*

12. Name it `ProductContext.cs`.

13. Now, open the `appsettings.json` file and add the following code:

```
"ConnectionStrings":
{
  "ProductConnection": "Data Source=.;Initial
  Catalog=ProductsDB;Integrated
  Security=True;MultipleActiveResultSets=True"
}
```

14. Right-click on the project in **Solution Explorer** and select **Manage NuGet Package**.

15. Under **NuGet Package Manager** screen, search for `Swashbuckle.ASPNETCore` and install it.

16. Add a new folder called `Persistence`.

17. Add an `IProductRepository` interface under the `Persistence` folder.

18. Add the following code to the `IProductRepository` interface:

```
namespace Chap08_02.Persistence
{
  public interface IProductRepository
  {
    void Add(Product product);
    IEnumerable<Product> GetAll();
    IEnumerable<Product> GetByProduct(string id);
    IEnumerable<Product> GetBy(string productName);
    void Remove(string id);
    void Update(Product product);
  }
}
```

Refer to the GitHub repository link at `https://github.com/`
`PacktPublishing/Building-RESTful-Web-Services-with-DotNET-`
`Core` for the complete source code.

19. Add the `ProductRepository.cs` class under the `Persistence` folder.

20. Add the following code to `ProductRepository.cs`:

```
public IEnumerable<Product> GetByProduct(string id) =>
_context.Products.FromSql("SELECT * FROM dbo.Products WHERE id="+
id).Include(p => p.Category)
    .ToList();
```

21. Open the `Startup.cs` file and add the following code:

```
services.AddScoped<IProductRepository, ProductRepository>();
services.AddDbContext<ProductContext>
(
  o => o.UseSqlServer
  (
    Configuration.GetConnectionString("ProductConnection")
  )
);
services.AddSwaggerGen
(
  swagger =>
  {
    swagger.SwaggerDoc("v1", new Info { Title = "Product APIs",
    Version = "v1"
  });
});
```

22. Now, you are ready to play with the application. Run the application from the menu or hit *F5*. In the web browser, add the /swagger suffix to the URL in the address bar, as shown in the following screenshot:

It will show the Swagger API documentation, as shown in the following screenshot:

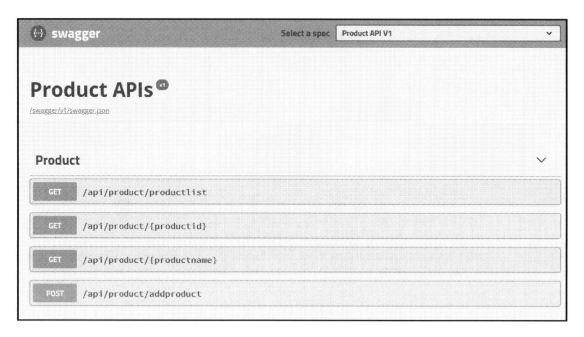

Swagger documentation for the Product APIs

 I used Swagger for the documentation and to test API calls. You can use other API test clients, such as Advanced Rest Client and PostMan.

23. To test our unsecured code, click on the `GET`
   `/api/product/{productid}` resource and pass the product ID, as shown in the
   following screenshot:

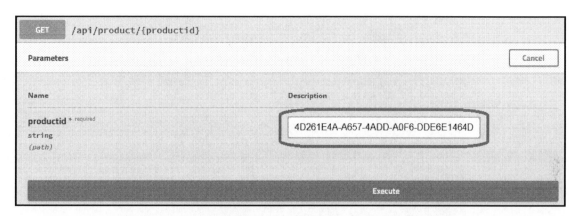

24. Click **Execute**. You should see the following expected output:

Request URL

```
http://localhost:42918/api/product/'4D261E4A-A657-4ADD-A0F6-DDE6E1464D55'
```

Server response

Code	Details
200	**Response body**

```json
[
  {
    "productId": "4d261e4a-a657-4add-a0f6-dde6e1464d55",
    "productName": "Learn C#",
    "productDescription": "Leanr C# in 7 days",
    "productImage": "csharp.jpeg",
    "productPrice": 520,
    "categoryId": "5ccaa9d0-e436-4d1e-a463-b45696d73a9f",
    "categoryName": "Books",
    "categoryDescription": "Technical Books"
  }
]
```

Now, let's try to add the OR clause and see what happens. Here, I am entering the productid value as 4D261E4A-A657-4ADD-A0F6-DDE6E1464D55 or 1=1. Execute it and look at the result:

```
[
    {
        "productId": "02341321-c20b-48b1-a2be-47e67f548f0f",
        "productName": "Microservices for .NET",
        "productDescription": "Microservices for .NET Core",
        "productImage": "microservices.jpeg",
        "productPrice": 651,
        "categoryId": "5ccaa9d0-e436-4d1e-a463-b45696d73a9f",
        "categoryName": "Books",
        "categoryDescription": "Technical Books"
    },
    {
        "productId": "4d261e4a-a657-4add-a0f6-dde6e1464d55",
        "productName": "Learn C#",
        "productDescription": "Leanr C# in 7 days",
        "productImage": "csharp.jpeg",
        "productPrice": 520,
        "categoryId": "5ccaa9d0-e436-4d1e-a463-b45696d73a9f",
        "categoryName": "Books",
        "categoryDescription": "Technical Books"
    }
]
```

Here, we can see that our application is affected by SQL injection. You are seeing all the records from the table. It happened because of the raw SQL query (refer to https://docs. microsoft.com/en-us/ef/core/querying/raw-sql for more information) that we are using. You can find the reason for the earlier results after looking closer at the code. The following screenshot will remind you what the request URL was:

```
Request URL

http://localhost:42918/api/product/'4D261E4A-A657-4ADD-A0F6-DDE6E1464D55'%20or%201%3D1
```

This is the injected URL. When our repository's `GetByProduct(string id)` method executed, it created the following raw SQL query:

```
SELECT [p].[Id], [p].[CategoryId], [p].[Description], [p].[Image],
[p].[Name],
 [p].[Price],[p.Category].[Id],[p.Category].[Description],
[p.Category].[Name]
FROM (SELECT * FROM dbo.Products WHERE id='4D261E4A-A657-4ADD-A0F6-
DDE6E1464D55' or 1=1) AS [p]
INNER JOIN [Categories] AS [p.Category] ON [p].[CategoryId] =
[p.Category].[Id]
```

This shows that the attacker did the job very smartly and quietly. Our unsecured code bled and returned the entirety of the data of the targeted table. I used the SQL profiler (`https://docs.microsoft.com/en-us/sql/tools/sql-server-profiler/sql-server-profiler`) to trace the queries.

Fixing SQL injection attacks

There is nothing more dangerous than unsecured code. With unsecured code, the application is always in danger. Attackers can steal data at any time, forcefully manipulating things by tampering with requests.

 Saineshwar Bageri has written 10 tips for creating a secure ASP.NET web application. You can read them at `https://www.codeproject.com/Articles/1116318/Points-to-Secure-Your-ASP-NET-MVC-Applications`.

You can stop an SQL injection attack with the following two techniques:

- **Validations**: We will discuss these later in the chapter.
- **Using parameters in raw SQL queries**: This is in addition to using a raw SQL query directly by concatenating values (refer to our example of unsecured code). In this way, you can rewrite the `GetByProduct(string id)` method as the following:

```
public IEnumerable<Product> GetByProduct(string id) =>
_context.Products
    .FromSql("SELECT * FROM dbo.Products WHERE id={0}", id)
    .Include(p => p.Category)
    .ToList();
```

The preceding code still contains a raw SQL query, but it is secure enough to handle any injected code. If you try the same parameter value we used earlier, then the modified code will not accept it. It will throw an exception, as shown in the following screenshot:

```
public IEnumerable<Product> GetByProduct(string id) => _context.Products
    .FromSql("SELECT * FROM dbo.Products WHERE id={0}", id)
    .Include(p => p.Category)
    .ToList();    ⊗
```

Exception User-Unhandled   ⊟ ✕

System.Data.SqlClient.SqlException: 'Conversion failed when converting from a character string to uniqueidentifier.'

View Details | Copy Details
▷ Exception Settings

You can also use string the interpolation syntax with a raw SQL query if your EF Core version is 2.0.0 or above. With string interpolation, the code looks like the following:

```
public IEnumerable<Product> GetByProduct(string id) =>
_context.Products
.FromSql($"SELECT * FROM dbo.Products WHERE id={id}")
.Include(p => p.Category)
.ToList();
```

- **Data encryption**: We will discuss this later in the chapter.

Cross-site request forgery

Cross-site request forgery (CRSF) can also be shortened to **XSRF**. This is a common attack where the attacker infuses an unwanted action while the client is interacting (request/response) with the hosted application. Generally, attackers use malicious code to influence the interaction.

Malicious code is scripting code that downloads onto a web browser and executes, even without the knowledge of the authenticated user. For details, refer to `https://www.techopedia.com/definition/4013/malicious-active-content`.

Attackers are very smart, and they use different platforms to provide spurious links to malicious code. These links are very similar to the domain (website) that is under attack. Financial websites are the main targets.

The following diagram depicts an XSRF attack:

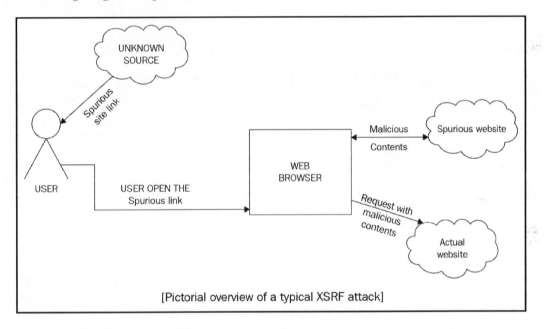

[Pictorial overview of a typical XSRF attack]

Attackers could send a link via email, social media, or any other medium. When the user clicks on the link, he or she will be in the world of the attacker without knowing that it's a spurious site and not their intended site.

 You can find the official web page at `https://docs.microsoft.com/en-us/aspnet/core/security/anti-request-forgery`.

CSRF vulnerabilities are fundamentally a problem with the web app, not the end user.

To handle this kind of attack, you need to build a system that is secure and properly authenticated. I will walk you through the details in the coming section focusing on authentication.

Authentication and authorization in action

Up until now, you have learned about the basics of authentication and authorization. In this section, you will see these two most important ways of securing an application in action.

Basic authentication, token-based authorization, and other authentications

Whenever you're talking about secured web services/web applications, you should think about the all the points I mentioned regarding authentication and authorization in the previous sections.

In this section, I'm going to discuss authentication and authorization at the implementation stage.

Basic authentication

As is evident from the word *basic*, basic authentication involves a mechanism where the system asks for simple credentials (username and password) to authenticate or validate the user via incoming requests from the client to the web or application servers via RESTful web services (in our case, ASP.NET Core web APIs).

Consider the following diagram, which showcases basic authentication:

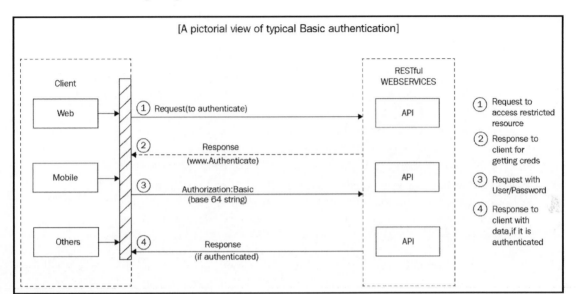

The preceding diagram is of the basic HTTP authentication that I'm going to implement in our code. Here, the request comes from the client to access resources that are protected (resources that are kept from public access). The request contains a username and password in its header at the service end, and the service checks whether it is a validate request or not by validating the username and password from its repository, usually a database store. The service returns the data in its response to the client if the user is validated; otherwise, it returns invalid credentials with HTTP status code 401.

You can find a complete list of HTTP status codes, along with their definitions, at `https://www.w3.org/Protocols/rfc2616/rfc2616-sec10.html`.

The security concerns of basic authentication

Basic authentication, as its name suggests, is a very basic authentication mechanism, and is not too secure when it comes to stopping attackers. Here, I have jotted down the following security vulnerabilities in the authentication process:

- **Credentials**: The required credentials are the most important security concern that could lead to security breaches, which could in turn further exploit the system's weak security.
- **Request**: Requests can be tampered with, and could lead to a big security breach; with basic authentication, every request carries the credentials (username and password), which can be tampered with and used to further exploit the system.
- **Closing the browser session**: There is a concern that should be high priority—there is no ability to log out from an application using the basic authentication method, unless the user closes the browser to destroy the browser session themselves.

You can look at the official web page at `https://docs.microsoft.com/en-us/aspnet/web-api/overview/security/basic-authentication` for more information.

> *"Basic authentication is also vulnerable to CSRF attacks. After the user enters credentials, the browser automatically sends them on subsequent requests to the same domain, for the duration of the session."*

There might be more security concerns that make the basic authentication mechanism the weakest with respect to web application security.

 Basic authentication leads to various security concerns. I am not going to showcase these using code examples of basic authentication, but if you still want to test the basic authentication mechanism, then I suggest that you extract the code from the forked GitHub repository at `https://github.com/garora/Bazinga.AspNetCore.Authentication.Basic`.

Token-based authorization

I explained authorization in the earlier sections of this chapter, where you saw that authorization is the next step after authentication to access restricted resources.

Let's consider the following diagram, which depicts token-based authentication:

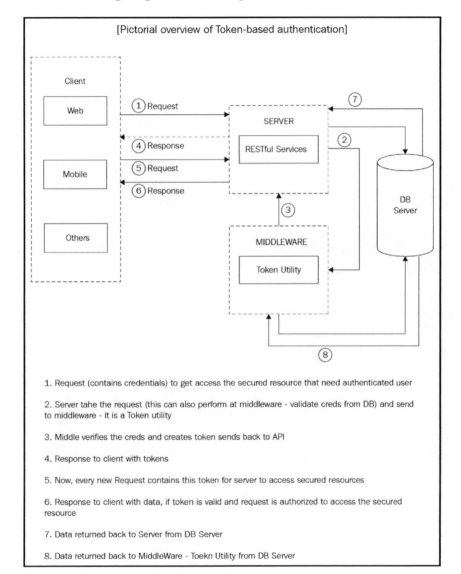

1. Request (contains credentials) to get access the secured resource that need authenticated user

2. Server tahe the request (this can also perform at middleware - validate creds from DB) and send to middleware - it is a Token utility

3. Middle verifies the creds and creates token sends back to API

4. Response to client with tokens

5. Now, every new Request contains this token for server to access secured resources

6. Response to client with data, if token is valid and request is authorized to access the secured resource

7. Data returned back to Server from DB Server

8. Data returned back to MiddleWare - Toekn Utility from DB Server

The preceding diagram shows a token-based authentication. If the request is verified (depending upon the identification of the credentials), then the client sends a request with the credentials and the returned token. The client then stores this token. It then sends these tokens with the headers in every request until the token is valid. If it is authorized to access the secure resource, the server verifies the request check and responds with the data. In some cases, the client may request a new token or call a refresh token if the existing token expires.

Let's add an `AuthRequet` model, as shown in our API project created in the previous sections:

```
public class AuthRequest
{
  public string UserName { get; set; }
  public string Password { get; set; }
}
```

Add a new `GenerateTokenController.cs` controller in the `Controller` folder. Here is our `GetToken` POST resource:

```
[AllowAnonymous]
[HttpPost]
public IActionResult RequestToken([FromBody] AuthRequest request)
{
  //Kept it simple for demo purpose
  var user = _loginRepository.GetBy(request.UserName,
  request.Password);
  if (user == null) return BadRequest("Invalid credentials.");
  var token = new TokenUtility().GenerateToken
  (
    user.UserName,
    user.Id.ToString());
    return Ok(new
    {
      token = new JwtSecurityTokenHandler().WriteToken(token)
    }
  );
}
```

Did you notice the `[AllowAnonymous]` attribute in the preceding code? You will see it in later sections. In the preceding code, I simply validate the credentials, and if the credentials are valid, the `TokenUtility` middleware generates the token.

Here is the `TokenUtility` code:

```
public JwtSecurityToken GenerateToken(string userName, string userId)
{
  var claims = new[]
  {
    new Claim(JwtRegisteredClaimNames.Sub, userName),
    new Claim(JwtRegisteredClaimNames.Jti, userId)
  };
  var key = new SymmetricSecurityKey(Encoding.UTF8.GetBytes(JwtKey));
  var creds = new SigningCredentials(key,
  SecurityAlgorithms.HmacSha256);
  var token = new JwtSecurityToken(TokenIssuer,
  TokenIssuer,
  claims,
  expires: DateTime.Now.AddMinutes(30),
  signingCredentials: creds);
  return token;
}
```

The preceding code is self-explanatory: it generates the token. In this code, I put `JwtKey` as a constant (for demonstration purposes only).

> In production, `JwtKey` should be kept in the environment variable (for security reasons) and can be easily accessible, as in, for example, `string jwtKey = Environment.GetEnvironmentVariable("JwtKey");`.

I am not going to discuss the repository model and other such approaches as these are self-explanatory. You can extract the entire source code from the GitHub repository at `https://github.com/PacktPublishing/Building-RESTful-Web-Services-with-DotNET-Core`.

To enable token-based authentication, you need to make a few changes in the `startup.cs` file by inserting Add `app.UseAuthentication();` in the `Configure` method before `app.UseMvc();`.

In the `ConfigureService` method, add the following code:

```
services.AddAuthentication()
.AddJwtBearer(cfg =>
{
  cfg.RequireHttpsMetadata = false;
  cfg.SaveToken = true;
  cfg.TokenValidationParameters = new TokenValidationParameters()
  {
    ValidIssuer = "gaurav-arora.com",
```

```
        ValidAudience = "gaurav-arora.com",
        IssuerSigningKey = new
        SymmetricSecurityKey
        (
          Encoding.UTF8.GetBytes("abcdefghijklmnopqrstuvwxyz")
        )
    };
});
```

Build and run the project. Let's do a simple test using the Swagger documentation, as shown in the following screenshot:

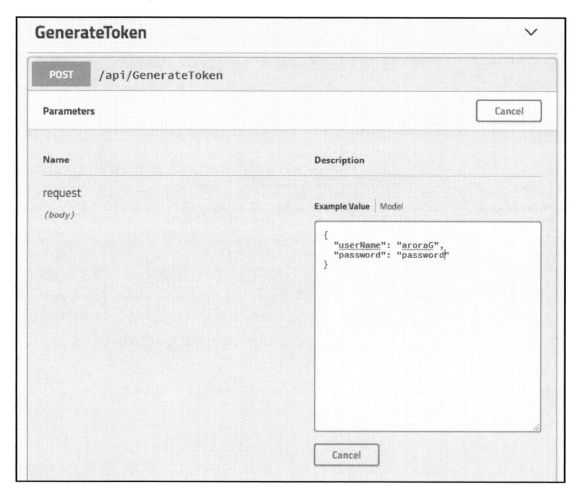

This will give the token upon a valid request:

```
{
  "token":
"eyJhbGciOiJIUzI1NiIsInR5cCI6IkpXVCJ9.eyJzdWIiOiJhcm9yYUciLCJqdGkiOiIxMDI3MjlkN1liZTk4LTRjMTUtOWRkNC8yZDcwOWFjFjZmQzYzgiLCJleHAiOjE1MjRkNTIyOTEsImlzcyI6ImdhdXJhdj11
hcm9yYS5jb20iLCJhdWQiOiJnYXVyYXYtYXJvcmEuY29tEuY29tIn0.eScNlxjDY_zU0ggd6aU5KH2s3ZNcPZ_7cBxJV3Yu3cI"
}
```

We will make a complex authorization process to access resources depending on the roles and access levels of the users in the coming sections.

Other authentication methods

Apart from basic and token-based authentications, you can also go with other available authentication mechanisms (we will not discuss these in detail, as they are beyond the scope of this book). IdentityServer4 is one of the most famous authentication servers and enables authentication as a service, single sign-in/sign-out, and many more options (refer to `https://identityserver4.readthedocs.io/en/release/` for more information).

Securing services using annotations

ASP.NET Core provides various ways to make secure application annotations (data annotations). This option is one of the ways in which we can secure our models for a web application. Data annotations provide a way to validate the inputs at the client end or the server end.

Validations

It is self-explanatory from the name *validations* that they are nothing but validators of user/client inputs. The user input can be validated at the client end or at the API end (server side). In RESTful services, you can validate the input using model validations with the help of data annotations.

 If the model is validated, this does not guarantee that data that comes with the request is safe.

In this section, we will rewrite our model used in the code example of the previous section.

Here is the modified `ProductViewModel` code:

```
public class ProductViewModel
{
   public Guid ProductId { get; set; }
   [Required]
   public string ProductName { get; set; }
   [Required]
   public string ProductDescription { get; set; }
   public string ProductImage { get; set; }
   [Required]
   public decimal ProductPrice { get; set; }
   [Required]
   public Guid CategoryId { get; set; }
   public string CategoryName { get; set; }
   public string CategoryDescription { get; set; }
}
```

Do not forget to include the `System.ComponentModel.DataAnnotations` namespace while using annotations.

In the preceding code, I used a very simple annotation, the `required` attribute. This makes sure that our model has the required properties.

Here is our `Post` resource to add a new product item:

```
[HttpPost]
[Route("addproduct")]
public IActionResult Post([FromBody] ProductViewModel productvm)
{
   if (productvm == null)
   return BadRequest();
   var productModel = ToProductModel(productvm);
   _productRepository.Add(productModel);
   return StatusCode(201, Json(true));
}
```

Compile the application and run it to test the impact of the data annotation on our model. This time, you can try this using PostMan (https://getpostman.com/) to test the API.

The following screenshot shows the `addproduct POST` resource; the `/api/product/addproduct` API is used to save the product:

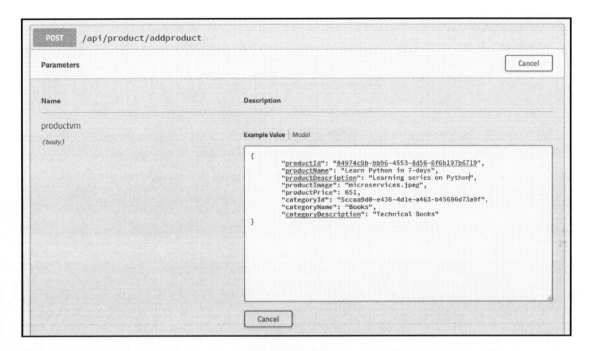

POST request using Swagger

The preceding input is valid; you have supplied all the required values. Let's remove `Price` and `ProductName`. You will see that there is no change while you execute the request, even without supplying the required values. Here, the validation failed. The reason why these data annotations did not affect the process is that you did not direct the system to validate the input. To validate the input, you should tell the system explicitly what you want to validate, for example, the model state. We will fix this with the help of filters in the coming section.

Securing context

With the help of the `filter` attribute, you can implement security at the context level. In this section, we will rewrite our model and API resources to implement filters/attributes.

In the previous section, we used the `Required` attribute with our `Product` model, and this did not work for us. In this section, we will fix the problem with the help of filters (for more information on filters, go to `https://docs.microsoft.com/en-us/aspnet/core/mvc/controllers/filters`).

Lets add a custom filter that validates the input, detecting whether any of the required fields are missing. If they are, it will just throw an exception. You need to modify the previous code, changing the Product model to the following:

```
[Required(ErrorMessage = "Product Name shoud not be empty.")]
public string ProductName { get; set; }
```

Simply add ErrorMessage in the required ProductName field; the rest of the properties of the model remain unchanged.

Now, add a new Filters folder in the project from **Solution Explorer.** To do this, go through the steps we followed in the previous section on *SQL injections* and add a new class in this folder named ValidateInputAttribute.cs using the following code:

```
namespace Chap08_04.Filters
{
  public class ValidateInputAttribute : ActionFilterAttribute
  {
    public override void OnActionExecuting(ActionExecutingContext
    context)
    {
      if (!context.ModelState.IsValid)
      context.Result = new BadRequestObjectResult
      (context.ModelState);
    }
  }
}
```

Apply this filter as an attribute to the Post resource to add the product. Our code should look like the following:

```
[HttpPost]
[Route("addproduct")]
[ValidateInput]
public IActionResult Post([FromBody] ProductViewModel productvm)
{
  if (productvm == null)
  return BadRequest();
  var productModel = ToProductModel(productvm);
  _productRepository.Add(productModel);
  return StatusCode(201, Json(true));
}
```

Run the application and enter the new product values without the product name, as shown in the following screenshot:

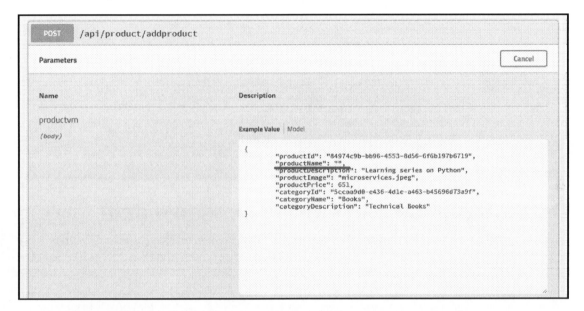

Process the request and look at the response from the server, shown in the preceding screenshot. The request will not be processed, and a response will come from the server notifying you of a bad request with the relevant error message.

The following screenshot shows the **Bad Request** response (HttpStatus Code **400**):

Server response	
Code	**Details**
400 *Undocumented*	Error: Bad Request **Response body** ``` { "ProductName": ["Product Name shoud not be empty."] } ```

To make any filter available anywhere, you should add the following code in the `startup.cs` configure method, like this:

```
services.AddMvc(option =>
{
  option.Filters.Add(typeof(ValidateInputAttribute));
});
```

Now, let's come back to our token-based authorization method. In the previous application, you saw how we can build an API to validate the credentials. Now, let's make a policy to restrict a resource. A detailed explanation of this topic is beyond the scope of this book; I suggest that you refer to the official documentation at `https://docs.microsoft.com/en-us/aspnet/core/security/authorization/policies`.

Data encryption and storing sensitive data

Data security is always a big concern in any application, and it is a high priority while writing or designing applications. You can use any hashing algorithm to protect the data by encryption and decryption, but it would lead to a performance hit. ASP.NET Core provides a way to protect data with the help of the ASP.NET DataProtection (`https://www.nuget.org/packages/Microsoft.AspNetCore.DataProtection.Abstractions/`) NuGet package.

> A complete explanation of this topic is beyond the scope of this book. You can refer to `https://docs.microsoft.com/en-us/aspnet/core/security/data-protection/` for further information.

Sensitive data

While you work with APIs, you have to store sensitive data: the API key, secret key, username, password, and so on. The following are a few recommendations for you to take into consideration while you're working with this data in the ASP.NET Core application:

- You should separate the configuration files from code.
- You should avoid storing this data in plain text files.
- You can use a separate class file where you can store these data values in the form of constants.

- You should store confidential data in environment variables. For more information, refer to `http://www.dowdandassociates.com/blog/content/howto-set-an-environment-variable-in-windows-command-line-and-registry/`.
- You can also use a secret manager to store your confidential data (`https://docs.microsoft.com/en-us/aspnet/core/security/app-secrets?tabs=visual-studio#secret-manager`).

Sensitive data varies from application to application and requirement to requirement. For more details, you can refer to `https://stormpath.com/blog/store-protect-sensitive-data-dotnet-core`.

Summary

In this chapter, we have discussed data security, following the OWASP security standard, and looking at JWT authentication. We also discussed custom filters and input validations using a code example. Data protection is always a high priority for any web application. We discussed data protection methods when storing sensitive data in an ASP.NET Core application.

In the next chapter, we will discuss the performance of web services by looking at the scale-in, scale-out methodology and the implementation of a few caching mechanisms.

Scaling RESTful Services (Performance of Web Services)

9

In the world of the web, everyone is either writing or looking for a web application. As demand increases, every web application needs to be able to serve more requests—sometimes thousands of requests a day. Applications should therefore be written to handle this huge requests.

Say, as an example, that you are part of a development and support team that is responsible for developing the company's flagship product, FlixOne Store. This product is popular and gains traction, leading to your e-commerce website (FlixOne) being inundated with consumer traffic. The payment service in your system is slow, which has almost brought the whole thing down, causing you to lose customers. Although this is an imaginary scenario, it can happen in real life and can lead to a loss of business. To avoid such a scenario, you should think about the scalability of the FlixOne application.

 Scalability is one of the most important non-functional requirements for a critical system. Serving a couple of users with hundreds of transactions is not the same as serving millions of users with several million transactions.

In this chapter, we will discuss scalability in general. We'll also discuss how to scale RESTful services, what to consider when we design them, and how to avoid cascading failures using different patterns including techniques, libraries, and tools that can also be helpful for our regular applications.

By the end of this chapter, you will have learned about:

- Clustering
- Load balancing
- An introduction to scalability

Clustering

Clustering is a way to provide the same service on more than one server. With the addition of more servers, you can avoid uncontrolled situations, such as failovers, system crashes, and so on. In the context of databases, clustering refers to the ability of several server instances to connect with a single server. Fault tolerance and load balancing are two of the main advantages of clustering.

Load balancing

A load balancer is a useful tool when clustering. You can define a **load balance** as a device that helps to distribute network or application traffic within and across the cluster servers, and to improve the responsiveness of the application.

In implementation, a load balancer is placed between the client and the servers. It helps to balance multiple application requests across multiple servers. In the other words, a load balancer reduces individual server time and prevents application server failure.

How does it work?

A load balancer works to make sure that an application's server is available. If one application's server is unavailable, the load balancer redirects all new requests to the available servers, as illustrated in the following diagram:

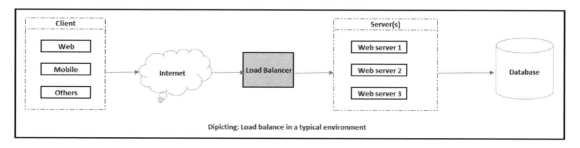

Dipicting: Load balance in a typical environment

In the preceding diagram, you can see a load balancer in its typical environment, where a system accepts multiple requests from different sources over the internet, which are then managed from multiple servers by the load balancer.

In .NET, this arrangement is also known as a web farm (`https://www.codeproject.com/Articles/114910/What-is-the-difference-between-Web-Farm-and-Web-Ga`).

A load balancer uses various algorithms, also known as load balancer methods: the least connection method, round-robin method, least response time method, least bandwidth method, least packets method, custom load method, and more.

A load balancer plays an important role in the scalability of an application as it makes sure that an application's server is available for server requests. Note that you will need to arrange your hardware infrastructure without a code change to cater for a load balancer (however, there will be some scenarios that call for a code change). There are a lot of load balancers on the market, such as Incapsula (`https://www.incapsula.com/`), F5 (`https://www.f5.com/`), Citrix Netscaler (`https://www.citrix.com/`), Dyn (`https://dyn.com/`), Amazon Elastic Load Balancing, and Amazon ELB (`https://aws.amazon.com/`).

In the coming sections, we will look at the different ways you can scale systems.

Introduction to scalability

Every application has its own ability to serve requests. An application's ability refers to its performance and how it meets its objectives when load is increased.

Many web applications refer to this as a number of requests in a stipulated time.

It's very important to make the right design decision when designing your web application; design decisions impact the scalability of your service. Be sure to strike the right balance so that your approach considers your services as well as their infrastructure, along with any need for scaling.

Performance and scalability are two different characteristics of a system. Performance deals with the throughput of the system, whereas scalability deals with serving the desired throughput for a larger number of users, or a larger number of transactions.

Scaling in (vertical scaling)

Scaling in or **scaling up** (also called **vertical scaling**) is a way of achieving scalability through the addition of more resources, such as memory or faster processors, to the same machine. This is not always applicable to all applications, as costing is also a factor when considering vertical scaling.

You can also upgrade your resources or hardware instead of adding new resources to your machine. For example, if you have 8 GB of RAM, you can upgrade it to 16 GB, and the same thing would be applicable for processors and other resources. Unfortunately, with upgrades in hardware, there is a limit to how much you can scale the machine. This may lead to simply shifting the bottleneck, rather than solving the real problem of improving scalability.

You can also migrate your application to an entirely different machine, such as simply migrating your application to a more powerful MacOS, for example.

 Scaling vertically does not involve any code changes so it is an easy task, but it does involve extra cost as it is quite an expensive technique. Stack Overflow is one of those rare examples of a .NET-based system that is scaled vertically.

Scaling out (horizontal scaling)

Scaling up, scaling out, or horizontal scaling adds more servers or nodes to service requests, rather than resources. If you do not want to scale up your application, there is always a way to scale it out.

Scaling out is a successful strategy when the application code does not depend on the server it is running on. However, if a request needs to be executed on a specific server, that is, if the application code has server affinity, it will be difficult to scale that out. In the case of stateless code, it is easier execute on any server. Hence, scalability is improved when stateless code is run on horizontally-scaled machines or clusters.

Due to the nature of horizontal scaling, it is a commonly used approach across the industry. There are many examples of large scalable systems managed in this way, such as Google, Amazon, and Microsoft.

Linear scalability

Linear scalability refers to scaling an application vertically with the application of Amdahl's law (`https://en.wikipedia.org/wiki/Amdahl%27s_law`). Here, you can also think about parallel computing.

> Parallel computing is a type of computing architecture that indicates simultaneous processing with the execution of several processors.

The benefits of linear scalability in your application include:

- No code changes are required
- Extra resources can be easily added
- There is physical availability

Distributed caching

With the help of distributed caching techniques, we can improve the scalability of our RESTful web services (web API). A distributed cache can be stored on multiple nodes of a cluster. A distributed cache enhances a web service's throughput, as the cache no longer requires an I/O trip to any external resource.

This approach has the following advantages:

- Clients get the same results
- The distributed cache is backed up by a persistence store and runs as a different remote process; even if the app server restarts or has any problems, it in no way affects the cache
- The source's data store has fewer requests made to it

Caching persisted data (data-tier caching)

Similar to application performance, you should also be considering database performance. By caching persisted data, you will get better performance after adding a caching layer to your database. This is also important when read requests are heavily used in an application. We will now take a look at EF Core's levels of caching as an example.

First-level caching

This is an inbuilt session cache enabled by EF Core. From the first request from a service, an object is retrieved from the database and is stored in an EF Core session. In other words, EF Object Context and DbContext maintain state information about the entities they are managing. As soon as the context is no longer available, its state information is also gone.

Second-level caching

Second-level caching is important for applications that have been developed in a mostly distributed manner or have-long running requests that need persisted data, such as web applications. Second-level caching exists outside the scope of a transaction or application, and these caches are available for any context or instance. You can use the caching mechanism available to your application instead of writing your own code, such as Memcached.

Application caching

Application caching or application-tier caching helps to cache any object in an application. This further improves the scalability of an application. In the following section, we will discuss the various caching mechanisms available.

CacheCow

CacheCow comes into the picture when you want to implement HTTP caching on both the client and server. This is a lightweight library and ASP.NET web API support is currently available. CacheCow is open source and comes with an MIT license that is available on GitHub (`https://github.com/aliostad/CacheCow`).

To get started with CacheCow, you need to get ready for both the server and client by taking the following steps:

1. Install the `Install-Package CacheCow.Server` NuGet package within your ASP.NET Web API project; this will be your server.
2. Install the `Install-Package CacheCow.Client` NuGet package within your client project; the client application will be WPF, Windows Form, Console, or any other web application.

3. Create a cache store. You need to create a cache

store
on the server side that requires a database for storing cache metadata (`https://github.com/aliostad/CacheCow/wiki/Getting-started#cache-store`).

Memcached

Memcached is an open source project that is customizable; you can use the source code and add to and update it as per your requirements. Memcached is defined by its official page (`https://memcached.org/`) as:

> *"An in-memory key-value store for small chunks of arbitrary data (strings, objects) from results of database calls, API calls, or page rendering."*

 Refer to `https://www.deanhume.com/memcached-for-c-a-walkthrough/` for a complete walkthrough.

Azure Redis Cache

Azure Redis Cache is built on top of an open source store called Redis (`https://github.com/antirez/redis`), which is an in-memory database and persists on disk. As per Microsoft's description (`https://azure.microsoft.com/en-in/services/cache/`):

> *"Azure Redis Cache is based on the popular open source Redis cache. It gives you access to a secure, dedicated Redis cache, managed by Microsoft and accessible from any application within Azure."*

Getting started with Azure Redis Cache is very simple if you take the following steps:

1. Create a web API project. Refer to our code example in previous chapters.
2. Implement Redis. For a referral point, use `https://github.com/StackExchange/StackExchange.Redis`. Also, install the `Install-Package StackExchange.Redis` NuGet package.

3. Update your config file for CacheConnection (`https://docs.microsoft.com/en-us/azure/redis-cache/cache-dotnet-how-to-use-azure-redis-cache#NuGet`).

4. Then, publish on Azure (`https://docs.microsoft.com/en-us/azure/redis-cache/cache-web-app-howto#publish-and-run-in-azure`).

Communication (asynchronous)

The term communication is self-explanatory; it is the act of interaction between services. Examples of this include the following:

- A service communicating with another service within the same application
- A service communicating with another service outside of the application (external services)
- A service communicating with a component (internal or external)

This communication happens over the HTTP protocol as messages or data traverse over the wire.

 Your application's performance impacts how services communicate with each other.

Asynchronous communication is one of the methods that help to scale applications. In ASP.NET Core, we can achieve this by using asynchronous HTTP calls (asynchronous programming): `https://docs.microsoft.com/en-us/dotnet/standard/asynchronous-programming-patterns/`

You should be careful with operations while handling asynchronous communications, for example, when adding a new product with an image. A system is designed so that it creates a thumbnail of the images in different sizes. This is a time-consuming task that could lead to a performance hit if handled incorrectly. From a design perspective, an asynchronous operation would not work in this scenario. Here, you should implement something like a task with a callback that tells the system when a job is complete. Sometimes, you may also require middleware to handle requests.

 The best way to implement asynchronous communication is with an asynchronous RESTful API.

When creating a scalable system, you must always think about asynchronous communication.

Summary

In this chapter, we discussed scalability, including the libraries available to help with it, tools, and so on. We then discussed how to scale RESTful services, what to consider when we design them, and how to avoid cascading failure using different patterns.

In the coming chapters, we will discuss and build a web client to call and consume RESTful services.

10
Building a Web Client (Consuming Web Services)

So far in this book, we have created RESTful services so that we can call or consume these services either within or from outside the project. In this chapter, we will discuss some use cases of these services, as well as the techniques and approaches for consuming RESTful web services.

In this chapter, we will cover the following topics:

- Consuming RESTful web services
- Building a REST web client

Consuming RESTful web services

Until now, we have created RESTful services and discussed server-side code with the help of code examples. We have consumed these services using external third-party tools, such as Postman and Advanced RESTClient. We have also consumed these services using fake objects and during unit testing. While helpful, these examples of consumption have not shown the true strength of RESTful services, as they have either tested their functionality or verified its output.

There may be situations where you will need to consume or use these services within another application similar to a controller, or even your own application itself. These applications can be any of the following:

- Console based
- Web based
- Mobile or any other device based

Let's take a look at one of the applications we've already discussed: let's say you need some mechanism to implement or consume an external API (in this case, PayPal) while integrating an online payment system. In this case, the external tools we've already covered, such as Postman and Advanced RESTClient can't help; to meet your needs, you require a REST client.

The following diagram illustrates how services can be consumed using a REST client with the help of an HTTP client. In the following diagram, the REST client is interacting (request, response) with both external and network services that have been developed in ASP.NET Core or are located on either the same or a different server.

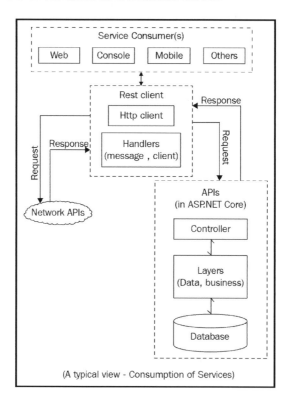

(A typical view - Consumption of Services)

Web, **Console**, **Mobile**, and so on, are the clients consuming these services with the help of the REST client.

We will now discuss how to build a REST client that we can use to consume other RESTful web services (that is, APIs) in our application.

Building a REST web client

RESTful services may or may not be a part of a web application. A web application may call or consume external APIs or services from the same application. The program that enables the interaction or communication (request, response) between the services and the application consuming those services is called a **client**.

 A client helps applications to communicate (Request, Response) with APIs.

In this section, we will create a web client. A web client is an application or program written in ASP.NET Core.

Before we build a test web client, we need to discuss what we have to call.

Continuing our example of the FlixOne BookStore, the following table lists the produces and services that we will call and consume:

API resource	Description
GET /api/product	Gets a list of products.
GET /api/product{id}	Gets a product.
PUT /api/product{id}	Updates an existing product.
DELETE /api/product{id}	Deletes an existing product.
POST /api/product	Adds a new product.

Our FlixOne product service is designed for the following tasks:

- Adding a new product
- Updating an existing product
- Deleting an existing product
- Retrieving a product

We have already ensured Swagger support for our product APIs (please refer to the previous chapters for more information), so let's get going. To start with this project, follow these steps:

1. First, run **Visual Studio 2017**
2. Select **File | Open**
3. Select the project **FlixOne.BookStore.ProductService**
4. Run the project by pressing *F5* or clicking directly from the menu
5. Enter the following URL: `http://localhost:10065/swagger/`

You should now see Swagger documentation for your **Product APIs**, as shown in the following screenshot:

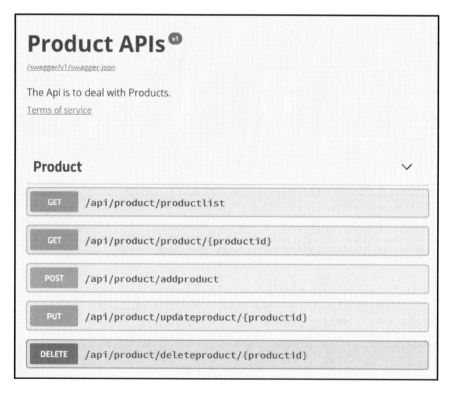

Product APIs documentation

Cooking the web client

We have already discussed what APIs need to consume and which resource returns what, so now it's time to cook our web client so we can consume and call our product APIs. To do so, follow these steps:

1. To create an entirely new solution for our new project, go to **File** | **New** | **Project** (or press *Ctrl + Shift + N*) as shown in the following screenshot.

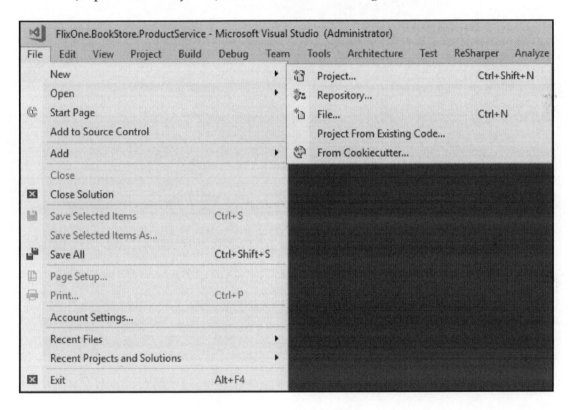

2. From **New Project,** select **ASP.NET Core Web Application**.

3. Name the project `FlixOne.BookStore.WebClient` and then click **OK** as shown in the following screenshot:

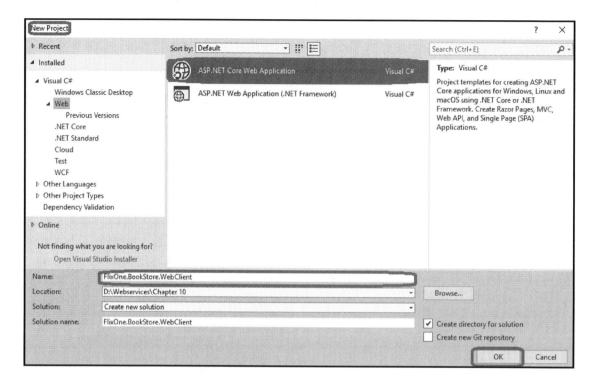

4. From the **ASP.NET Core** template window, select **Web Application** and click **OK** as shown in the following screenshot:

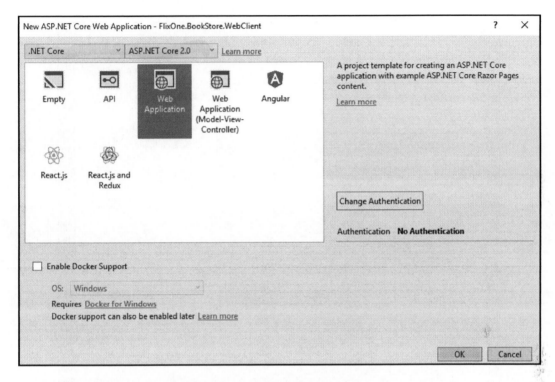

5. Now run the project **Debug | Start Debugging** or hit the *F5* key.
6. You should now see a default website template.
7. We will now create a web client using **RestSharp**. We need to add the support of RestSharp to get the facility to make a call over the HTTP protocol for our API resources.

> RestSharp is a lightweight HTTP client library. You can make changes to suit your needs, as it is an open source library. You can find the complete repository at `https://github.com/restsharp/RestSharp`

8. Add a NuGet package using **Open Package Manager** (right-click on **Solution** from **Solution Explorer**), as shown in the following screenshot:

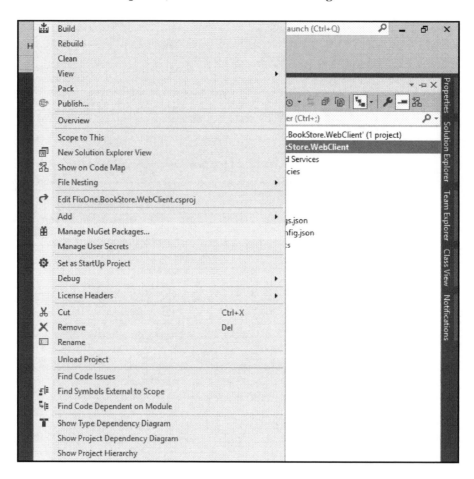

9. Search for **RestSharp** and check the checkbox saying **include prerelease**, and then click **Install** as shown in the following screenshot:

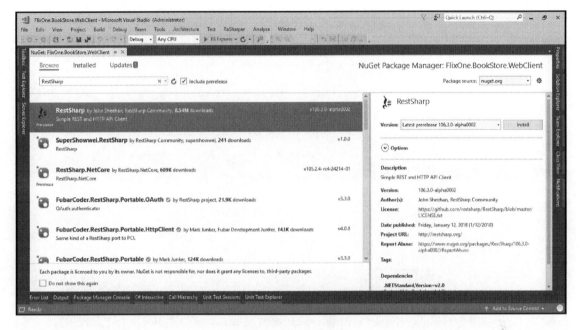

Selecting the RestSharp NuGet package

10. The required packages will now be installed, as shown in the following screenshot:

Installing the RestSharp package

Before going forward, let's first make sure that our product APIs are working correctly. Run the product API project, open Swagger, and hit a `GET /api/product/productlist` resource as follows:

After executing the previous resource, you should see a complete list of products, as shown in the following screenshot:

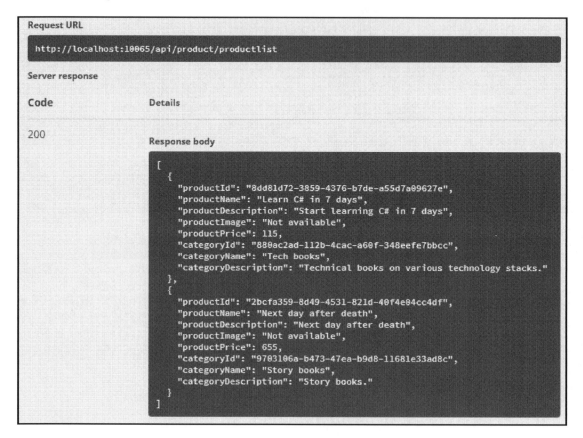

 Try all available resources to make sure that your product APIs are working correctly.

Writing code

So far, we have cooked the things required for writing code for our REST web client; in this section, we will be writing actual code:

1. Add a simple code to call or consume your product APIs.

If you created a new project in the same solution (refer to *step 1* of the section *Cooking the web client*), please make sure that the project Product API is running before you start your web client project.

2. Add a new class (*Ctrl* + *Shift* + *C*) in the `Client` folder and name it `RestSharpWebClient`.

3. Now open the `RestSharpWebClient` class and add the following code:

```
private readonly RestClient _client = new
RestClient("http://localhost:10065/api/");
```

The preceding code initializes RestClient of RestSharp and accepts the base URL as a string or a URI.

URI stands for Uniform Resource Identifier and is a representation of a string used to identify resources.

You may come across a scenario where there are multiple environments; in this case, you should store a URI where you point it as per your environment. For example, you can have the URI `http://devserver:10065/api/` for your development environment or the URI `http://testenv:10068/api/` for your QA environment. You should store these keys in the `config` file or somewhere similar so that the values are easily accessible. We recommend using `new RestClient(somevariableforURI);`.

 In our application, product APIs are running on localhost and the listening port `10065`. This may be different in your case.

Let's discuss the following code snippet to call or consume the `GET /api/product /productlist` resource and populate the complete product list, as follows:

```
public List<ProductViewModel> GetProducts()
{
  var request = new RestRequest("product/productlist", Method.GET);
  var response = _client.Execute<List<ProductViewModel>>(request);
  return response.Data ?? new List<ProductViewModel> {new
  ProductViewModel()};
}
```

Here, we are making a `GET` request using `RestRequest`, where we passed a resource and method.

To get a particular product using `productid`, enter the following code:

```
public ProductViewModel GetProductDetails(string productId)
{
  var request = new RestRequest("product/{productid}", Method.GET);
  request.AddParameter("productid", productId);
  var response = _client.Execute<ProductViewModel>(request);
  return response.Data ?? new ProductViewModel();
}
```

In the preceding code block, the `GetProductDetails` method does a similar thing to the method `GetProducts`. The difference is that it accepts the parameter `productId`.

The following is the complete code of our REST client:

```
public class RestSharpWebClient
{
  private readonly RestClient _client = new
  RestClient("http://localhost:10065/api/");
  public List<ProductViewModel> GetProducts()
  {
    var request = new RestRequest("product/productlist",
    Method.GET);
    var response = _client.Execute<List<ProductViewModel>>
    (request);
    //To avoid any exception lets return an empty view model
    //On production environment return exact exception or your
    custom code
    return response.Data ?? new List<ProductViewModel> {new
    ProductViewModel()};
  }
  public ProductViewModel GetProductDetails(string productId)
  {
    var request = new RestRequest("product/{productid}",
    Method.GET);
    request.AddParameter("productid", productId);
    var response = _client.Execute<ProductViewModel>(request);
    //To avoid any exception lets return an empty view model
    //On production environment return exact exception or your
    custom code
    return response.Data ?? new ProductViewModel();
  }
  public bool AddProduct(ProductViewModel product)
  {
    var request = new RestRequest("product/addproduct",
    Method.POST);
    request.AddBody(product);
    var response = _client.Execute(request);
    return response.StatusCode == HttpStatusCode.OK;
  }
  public bool UpdateProduct(string id, ProductViewModel product)
  {
    var request = new RestRequest("updateproduct", Method.PUT);
    request.AddQueryParameter("productid", id);
    request.AddBody(product);
    var response = _client.Execute(request);
    return response.StatusCode == HttpStatusCode.NoContent;
  }
  public bool DeleteProduct(string id, ProductViewModel product)
  {
    var request = new RestRequest("deleteproduct", Method.DELETE);
```

```
        request.AddQueryParameter("productid", id);
        request.AddBody(product);
        var response = _client.Execute(request);
        return response.StatusCode == HttpStatusCode.NoContent;
    }
}
```

With the preceding code snippet, you have now added the functionality that will call and consume your product APIs.

Implementing a REST web client

RESTful services may or may not be a part of your web application, but we still need to understand how to implement them.

So, now it's time to do some real work. Add `ProductController` to the project, as well as the following action:

```
public ActionResult Index()
{
  var webClient = new RestSharpWebClient();
  var products = webClient.GetProducts();
  return View("ProductList", products);
}
```

Take a look at the preceding code snippet. We have called the `GetProducts` method of `RestSharpWebClient` and populated our `Index.cshtml` view with a complete list of products.

To add another action method, enter the following complete code of our `ProductController`. The following code snippet contains the `Index` action method and gives us a list of products:

```
public class ProductController : Controller
{
  public ActionResult Index()
  {
    var webClient = new RestSharpWebClient();
    var products = webClient.GetProducts();
    return View("ProductList", products);
  }
  public ActionResult Details(string id)
  {
    var webClient = new RestSharpWebClient();
```

```
    var products = webClient.GetProductDetails(id);
    return View(products);
}
```

Let's now look at two Create action methods: HttpGet and HttpPost. The first one provides us with an entry screen for input and the second posts all the data (the input values) using the HttpPost method. On the server side, you can receive all data in an IFormCollection parameter, and you can also easily write logic to get all of your values in ProductViewModel.

```
public IActionResult Create()
{
    return View();
}
[HttpPost]
[ValidateAntiForgeryToken]
public IActionResult Create(IFormCollection collection)
{
    try
    {
        var product = new ProductViewModel
        {
            ProductId = Guid.NewGuid(),
            ProductName = collection["ProductName"],
            ProductDescription = collection["ProductDescription"],
            ProductImage = collection["ProductImage"],
            ProductPrice = Convert.ToDecimal(collection["ProductPrice"]),
            CategoryId = new Guid("77DD5B53-8439-49D5-9CBC-DC5314D6F190"),
            CategoryName = collection["CategoryName"],
            CategoryDescription = collection["CategoryDescription"]
        };
        var webClient = new RestSharpWebClient();
        var producresponse = webClient.AddProduct(product);
        if (producresponse)
        return RedirectToAction(nameof(Index));
        throw new Exception();
    }
    catch
    {
        return View();
    }
}
```

You can also write a `HttpPost` method that accepts a parameter of the type `ProductViewModel`.

The following code snippet shows us the code for the `Edit` action method, which is similar to the `Create` action method but except that it updates existing data rather than inserting new data:

```
public ActionResult Edit(string id)
{
  var webClient = new RestSharpWebClient();
  var product = webClient.GetProductDetails(id);
  return View(product);
}
[HttpPost]
[ValidateAntiForgeryToken]
public ActionResult Edit(string id, IFormCollection collection)
{
  try
  {
    var product = new ProductViewModel
    {
      ProductId = new Guid(collection["ProductId"]),
      ProductName = collection["ProductName"],
      ProductDescription = collection["ProductDescription"],
      ProductImage = collection["ProductImage"],
      ProductPrice = Convert.ToDecimal(collection["ProductPrice"]),
      CategoryId = new Guid(collection["CategoryId"]),
      CategoryName = collection["CategoryName"],
      CategoryDescription = collection["CategoryDescription"]
    };
    var webClient = new RestSharpWebClient();
    var producresponse = webClient.UpdateProduct(id, product);
    if (producresponse)
    return RedirectToAction(nameof(Index));
    throw new Exception();
  }
  catch
  {
    return View();
  }
}
```

The `Delete` action method is meant to remove a specific record or data from a database or collection. The action method `Delete` of `HttpGet` fetches a record based on a given ID and displays the data ready for modification. Another `Delete` action of `HttpPost` sends modified data to the server for further processing. This means the system can delete data and records.

```
public ActionResult Delete(string id)
{
  var webClient = new RestSharpWebClient();
  var product = webClient.GetProductDetails(id);
  return View(product);
}
[HttpPost]
[ValidateAntiForgeryToken]
public ActionResult Delete(string id, IFormCollection collection)
{
  try
  {
    var product = new ProductViewModel
    {
      ProductId = new Guid(collection["ProductId"]),
      ProductName = collection["ProductName"],
      ProductDescription = collection["ProductDescription"],
      ProductImage = collection["ProductImage"],
      ProductPrice = Convert.ToDecimal(collection["ProductPrice"]),
      CategoryId = new Guid(collection["CategoryId"]),
      CategoryName = collection["CategoryName"],
      CategoryDescription = collection["CategoryDescription"]
    };
    var webClient = new RestSharpWebClient();
    var producresponse = webClient.DeleteProduct(id, product);
    if (producresponse)
    return RedirectToAction(nameof(Index));
    throw new Exception();
  }
  catch
  {
    return View();
  }
}
}
```

Now let's open `_Layout.cshtml` from the `Shared` folder and add the following line to add a link to our newly added `ProductController`:

```
<li><a asp-area="" asp-controller="Product" asp-action="Index">Web
Client</a></li>
```

You should see a new menu named **Web Client** when you run the project, as shown in the following screenshot:

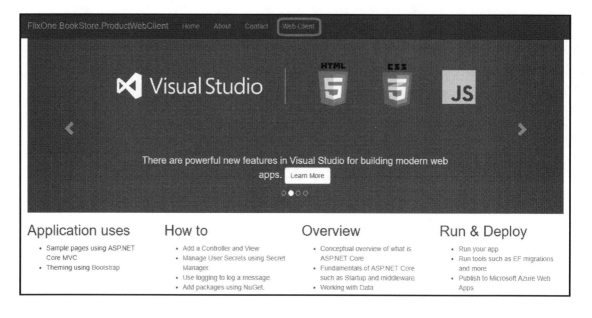

We are now ready to see some results. Click on the **Web Client** menu, and you will see the following screen:

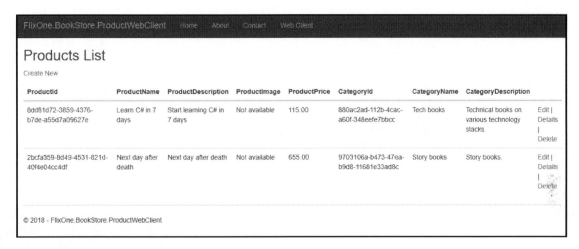

From the preceding screen, you can perform other operations, as well as call and consume your product APIs—namely, **Create**, **Edit**, and **Delete**.

Summary

The creation of RESTful services is important for any project, but these services are of no use if there is no way of using them. In this chapter, we looked at how to add RestSharp support to our web project and consume our pre-developed product APIs. We also created a web client that could consume web services by rendering output on our web pages using ASP.NET Core.

In the next chapter, we will discuss the hot topic of microservices, the next level of the separation of services. We will discuss how microservices communicate, what their advantages are, and why we require them.

11
Introduction to Microservices

So far, we have walked through the RESTful APIs with hands-on examples and created small applications. In the previous chapter, we developed an application and discussed the RESTful API, security, testing, performance, and deployment.

This chapter covers a brief introduction to microservices, which is the next stop on our RESTful services journey. In this chapter, we will cover the basic components of microservices and use an example of a monolithic application that is being converted into microservices.

We will cover the following topics:

- What are microservices?
- Communication in microservices
- Microservices testing strategy
- Scalability
- Microservices ecosystem in ASP.NET Core

Overview of microservices

In simple words, when one divides an application or a module into smaller, independent services, the outcome is also known as **microservices**. These small pieces can also be deployed independently.

If we go back in history, we find that the term microservices was used for the first time in 2011 at the workshop of Software Architects. In March 2012, James Lewis presented some of his ideas about the term microservices. By the end of 2013, various groups in the IT industry had started discussing microservices, and by 2014, microservices had become popular enough to be considered a serious contender for large enterprises.

So, what are microservices really? There are a plethora of definitions so you can define microservices as per your own understanding of the term or what kind of use cases and discussions you may have. Let us look at a microservices definition according to an official website: (source: `https://docs.microsoft.com/en-us/azure/service-fabric/service-fabric-overview-microservices`)

> *"Microservice applications are composed of small, independently versioned, and scalable customer-focused services that communicate with each other over standard protocols with well-defined interfaces."*

Microservice attributes

In the previous section, we saw that microservices are completely independent of other services in the system and run in their own processes. As per this definition, there are certain attributes that define microservices to be completely independent from other components. Let's first look at what the core attributes are:

- **Isolated functionality**: Don't try to achieve too much within a single microservice. Instead, design it for only one reason and do that well. This means that the design should try and avoid any dependency on any other part of the functionality. This part is extremely important in my opinion as it lays the foundation for the rest of the attributes.
- **Isolated data and state**: Each service owns its data and its state. It does not share ownership with any other application or part.
- **Independent deployment**: A cumulative effect of the preceding points. This helps you with continuous deployment.
- **Technology adoption**: This is easier when the first two points have been taken care of, since there is no longer an impact on any of the existing modules. The beauty here lies in the fact that you could have two different versions of a microservice in two different technologies. Extremely beneficial.
- **Consistency and resiliency**: It has to be impeccable. If you can't rely on a service to return within a speculated period or rely on it to be always available, then the whole purpose of it is lost.

Understanding microservice architecture

We have already discussed how the microservice architecture is a way to develop a single application containing a set of smaller services. These services are independent and run in their own processes.

In other words, we can say that microservices are a way to segregate our services so they can be handled independently of each other for design, development, deployment, and upgrade purposes.

Microservices have a lot of benefits, which are as follows:

- **Smaller codebase**: Each service is small, therefore easier to develop and deploy as a unit
- **Ease of independent environment**: With the separation of services, all developers work independently, deploy independently, and no one is bothered about any module dependencies

Communication in microservices

It is very important to consider the choice of messaging mechanisms carefully when dealing with a microservice architecture. If this one aspect is ignored, then it can compromise the entire purpose of designing with a microservices architecture.

Let's move ahead and consider our choices for both synchronous and asynchronous messaging along with different messaging formats.

Synchronous messaging

When a timely response is expected from a service by a system and the system waits on it till a response is received from the service, it is called **synchronous messaging**. REST is one of the most sought-after choices in a microservice architecture. It is simple and supports HTTP request-response, therefore there is no need to look for an alternative. This is also one of the reasons that most implementations of microservices use HTTP (API-based styles).

Asynchronous messaging

When a system is not immediately expecting a response from the service and it can continue processing without blocking the call, it is called as **asynchronous messaging**.

Message formats

Over the past few years, working with MVC and the like has got me hooked on the JSON format. You could also consider XML. Both these formats would do fine on HTTP with API style resource. Binary message formats are also available in case you need to use one. We are not recommending any formats here, you can go with any selected message format.

Why we should use microservices

Tremendous patterns and architectures have been explored, with some gaining popularity and others losing the battle for internet traffic. Each solution has its own advantages and disadvantages so it has become increasingly important for companies to respond quickly to fundamental demands such as scalability, high performance, and easy deployment. Any single aspect found not to be cost-effective could easily impact large businesses negatively, making the difference between a profitable and an unprofitable venture. The following diagram highlights the advantages of opting Microservices:

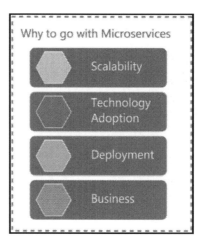

This is where we see microservices coming to the rescue of enterprise system architects. They can ensure their designs don't have any problems with the help of this architectural style. It is also important to consider the fact that this objective is met in a cost-effective and timely manner.

How a microservice architecture works

In previous sections, we discussed the microservice architecture and tried to shine more light on this term. Now, you can see how a microservices architecture might work; you can use any combination according to your own design approach. Here are a few points to remember when working on a microservice architecture:

- It is programming for the modern era, where we should follow all SOLID principles. It's object-oriented programming (OOP).
- It is the best way to expose functionality to other or external components so any programming language can use the functionality without adhering to any user interfaces or services (web services, API, REST services, and so on.)
- The whole system works in collaboration, which is not interconnected and interdependent.
- Each component is responsible for its own functionality.
- It segregates code. Segregated code is reusable.

Advantages of microservices

The following are some advantages of microservices:

- You don't have to invest to make the entire application scalable. In terms of a shopping cart, we could simply load balance the product search module and order-processing module while leaving less frequently used operation services such as inventory management, order cancellation, and delivery confirmation.
- We can easily match an organization's departmental hierarchies. With different departments sponsoring product development in large enterprises this can be a huge advantage.
- As the code is already done in a way that it is not dependent on code from other modules with isolated functionality, if done right, then the chances of a change in one microservice affecting another microservice is very small.

- Since the entire application is more like a group of ecosystems that are isolated from each other – we can deploy one microservice at a time if required. Failure of any one service need not bring the entire system down.
- You could port a single microservice or a whole bunch of them overnight to a different technology without your users even knowing it. And it goes without saying that you need to maintain those service contracts.
- Comes implied but a word of caution is necessary here. Make sure that your asynchronous call is used well and synchronous ones are not really blocking the whole flow of information. Use data partitioning well. We will come to this a little later, so don't worry now.
- In a competitive world, it is a definite advantage as users tend to lose interest quickly if you are slow to respond to new feature requests or the adoption of a new technology within your system.

Prerequisites of a microservice architecture

After the adoption of a microservice architecture is agreed upon, it is wise to have the following prerequisites in place:

- Requirements become more demanding with a quicker turnaround from development. It requires you to deploy and test as quickly as you can. If it is just a small number of services, then it is not a problem. However, with the number of services going up this could very quickly challenge the existing infrastructure and practices. For example—your Q/A and staging environment may no longer suffice to test the number of builds that are coming back from the development team.
- As the application goes to the public domain, it won't be long before the age-old script of development versus Q/A is played out again. The difference this time is that the business is at stake. So, you need to be prepared to respond quickly in an automated manner to identify the root cause when required.
- With an increasing number of microservices, you will quickly need a way to monitor the functioning and health of the entire system for any possible bottlenecks or issues. Without a means of monitoring the status of the deployed microservices and the resultant business function, it is impossible for any team to take a proactive deployment approach.

Scaling

Scaling is one of the biggest challenges that any business faces when trying to cater to an increased user base.

Scalability is simply the capability of a system/program to handle a growing work. In other words, scalability is the ability of the system/program to scale.

The scalability of a system is its ability to handle an increasing/increased load of work. There are two main strategies or types of scalability in which we can scale our application.

Vertical scaling

In vertical scaling, we analyze our existing application to find out the parts of the modules that are causing the application to slow down due to higher execution time. Making the code more efficient could be one strategy, so less memory is consumed. This exercise of reducing memory consumption could be for a specific module or the whole application. On the other hand, due to obvious challenges involved in this strategy, instead of changing an application, we could add more resources to our existing IT infrastructure such as upgrading the RAM, adding more disk drives, and so on. Both of these paths in vertical scaling have a limit to how beneficial they are, as after a specific point in time—the resulting benefit would plateau out. It is important here to keep this fact in mind; this kind of scaling requires downtime.

Horizontal scaling

In horizontal scaling, we dig deeper into modules that are showing a higher impact on the overall performance. We look at factors such as high concurrency to enable our application to serve an increased user base. We would also implement load balancing to process a greater amount of work. The option of adding more servers to the cluster does not require downtime, which is a definite advantage. It can differ from case to case, so we need to check whether the additional costs of power, licenses, and cooling is worthwhile up to that point.

DevOps culture

With the help of DevOps, a team should emphasize the collaboration of the development team and another operational team. We should set up a system where development, Q/A, and the infrastructure teamwork in collaboration.

Automation

Infrastructure setup can be a very time-consuming job. A developer can be idle while the infrastructure is being readied for him. He or she will be waiting for some time before joining the team and contributing. The process of infrastructure setup should not stop a developer from becoming productive, as it would reduce overall productivity. This should be an automated process. With the use of Chef or PowerShell, we can easily create our virtual machines and quickly ramp up the developer count as and when required. In that way, our developer can be ready to start work from day one of joining the team.

Testing

Testing is a critical task of any application and its more complex when working with microservices. We have to divide our testing approach as follows:

- With adopt TDD, a developer is required to test his or her own code. The test is simply another piece of code that validates whether the functionality is working as intended. If any functionality is found to be not satisfying the test code, the corresponding unit test would fail. That functionality can be easily fixed as it is known where the problem is. In order to achieve this, we can utilize frameworks such as MSTest or unit tests.
- The Q/A team can use scripts to automate their tasks. They can create scripts by utilizing QTP or the Selenium framework.

Deployment

Deployment is a huge challenge. To overcome this, we can introduce CI. In this process, we need to set up a CI server. With the introduction of CI, the entire process is now automated. As soon as the code is checked in by any team member, using version control TFS or Git in our case, the CI process kicks into action. It ensures that the new code is built and unit tests are run along with the integration test. In both scenarios, a successful build or otherwise, the team is alerted of the outcome. This enables the team to respond quickly to issues.

Next, we have continuous deployment. Here, we introduce various environments, namely a development environment, a staging environment, a Q/A environment, and so on. Now, as soon as the code is checked-in by any team member, continuous integration kicks into action. It invokes unit/integration test suites, builds the system, and pushes it out to the various environments we have set up. In this way, the turnaround time of the development team to provide a suitable build for Q/A is reduced.

Microservices ecosystem in ASP.NET Core

Whenever I think about a microservices eco in an ASP.NET Core system I think about various small APIs, async programming, callbacks, event triggering, and so on. Actually, the ecosystem is much bigger and somehow more complex.

We have already discussed that the microservice architectural style is a way to create small and independent units of a big application. This is not possible without the use of various tools and utilities.

The following diagram is a pictorial overview of a typical microservices architectural style that depicts different client requests to various services and how this request validates:

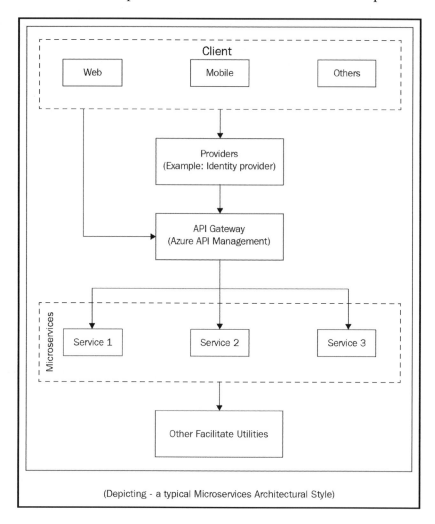

(Depicting - a typical Microservices Architectural Style)

A typical microservice ecosystem consists of the following components, you will get an idea about these components in ASP.NET Core in the sections ahead.

Azure Service Fabric – microservice platform

A platform is a must-have component for any ecosystem. It supports the system, works smoothly, and produces the expected results. Azure Service Fabric is simply a platform provided by Microsoft and it is very popular in the microservice ecosystem. It provides container deployment and orchestration.

Official documentation can be found at: `https://docs.microsoft.com/en-us/azure/service-fabric/service-fabric-overview`

> *"Azure Service Fabric is a distributed systems platform that makes it easy to package, deploy, and manage scalable and reliable microservices and containers."*

Stateless and Stateful services – a service programming model

A robust service programming model is the backbone of a microservices ecosystem. One should know what type of service model he/she should use as per his/her requirements:

- **Stateless**: Services do not persist any state between requests from the client. That is, the service doesn't know, nor care, that the subsequent request has come from the client that has/hasn't made the previous request. This is the best service programming model when we have external data storage. Our service can be based on a stateless service programming model that interacts and persists data on external database storage.
- **Stateful**: Services maintain a mutable state, actively processing or retaining state data that is specific to the task for which the service is meant.

Communication – a way to exchange data between services

If microservices are all about services then communication between services should be robust. Communication is a way to exchange data between services. Services communicate using Rest API (that is, HTTP calls request/response) and these are synchronous by nature.

When services communicate with each other they are actually exchanging data, also called messaging between services. It is very important to consider the choice of messaging mechanism carefully when dealing with a microservice architecture. If this one aspect is ignored, then it can compromise the entire purpose of designing with a microservice architecture. In monolithic applications, this is not a concern as the business functionality of components is invoked through function calls. On the other hand, this is happening via loosely coupled web-service-level messaging, where services are primarily based on SOAP. Microservice messaging mechanisms should be simple and lightweight.

There are no set rules for making a choice between various frameworks or protocols for a microservice architecture. However, there are a few points worthy of consideration here. Firstly, it should be simple enough to implement without adding any complexity to your system. Secondly, it should be lightweight enough, keeping in mind the fact that the microservice architecture could heavily rely on interservice messaging. Let's move ahead and consider our choices for both synchronous and asynchronous messaging along with different messaging formats.

Summary

The microservice architecture style provides certain benefits. It makes development quick and easy. It allows DevOps (CI and CD) teams to be separated geologically, work smoothly, and in sync. An application is divided into small service components or pieces so maintenance is easy. This allows the development team to let business sponsors choose what industry trends to respond to first. This results in cost benefits, better business responses, timely technology adoption, effective scaling, and removal of human dependence.

In this chapter, you have gained an idea of typical microservice architectural styles and microservice ecosystems in ASP.NET.

Now, I suggest you read the following on microservices to enhance your skills:

- *Building Microservices with .NET Core 2.0 – Second Edition* by PACKT (`https://www.packtpub.com/application-development/building-microservices-net-core-20-second-edition`)
- *Microservice Patterns and Best Practices* by PACKT (`https://www.packtpub.com/application-development/microservice-patterns-and-best-practices`)

Other Books You May Enjoy

If you enjoyed this book, you may be interested in these other books by Packt:

Building Microservices with .NET Core 2.0 - Second Edition
Gaurav Aroraa

ISBN: 9781788393331

- Get acquainted with Microsoft Azure Service Fabric
- Compare microservices with monolithic applications and SOA
- Learn Docker and Azure API management
- Define a service interface and implement APIs using ASP.NET Core 2.0
- Integrate services using a synchronous approach via RESTful APIs with ASP.NET Core 2.0
- Implement microservices security using Azure Active Directory, OpenID Connect, and OAuth 2.0
- Understand the operation and scaling of microservices in .NET Core 2.0
- Understand the key features of reactive microservices and implement them using reactive extensions

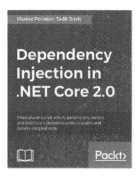

Dependency Injection in .NET Core 2.0
Marino Posadas, Tadit Dash

ISBN: 9781787121300

- Understand the concept of DI and its implications in modern software construction
- Learn how DI is already implemented in today's frameworks.
- Analyze how DI can be used with current software to improve maintainability and scalability.
- Learn the use of DI in .NET Core
- Get used to the possibilities that DI offers the ASP.NET Core developer in different scenarios.
- Learn about good practices and refactoring legacy code.

Leave a review - let other readers know what you think

Please share your thoughts on this book with others by leaving a review on the site that you bought it from. If you purchased the book from Amazon, please leave us an honest review on this book's Amazon page. This is vital so that other potential readers can see and use your unbiased opinion to make purchasing decisions, we can understand what our customers think about our products, and our authors can see your feedback on the title that they have worked with Packt to create. It will only take a few minutes of your time, but is valuable to other potential customers, our authors, and Packt. Thank you!

Index

Made in the USA
San Bernardino,
CA